Dear Annette, Love, Mercy

A Story of a Woman with Fortitude Who, Despite an
Unhappy Childhood and Traumatic Experiences,
Still Managed to Get on with Her Life and Enjoy It!

VIRGINIA LAGOS

Paperback: 978-1-963883-50-3
eBook: 978-1-963883-51-0
Library of Congress Control Number: 2024905621

Ordering Information:

Prime Seven Media
518 Landmann St.
Tomah City, WI 54660

Printed in the United States of America

Dedication

I dedicate this book to my mother, Mrs. Mercedes Marin and as a tribute in honor of her exemplary life.

Secondly, to my sons Anthony, Richard, and Victor, to whom I'd like to leave a legacy that they may know their roots and appreciate the value of leading a good life, as their grandmother did.

Acknowledgments

A big thank you to the wonderful people who inspired me to write this book:

My English teacher in high school, Mrs. Fely Wiedebush, who believed I had writing ability; Mrs. Carole Wilhelm, the daughter-in-law of Mom's pen pal, who kindly sent me an album of some of Mom's handwritten letters to her mother-in-law Mrs. Annette Wilhelm; Mr. Paul Hughes, who encouraged me and was my accountabilibuddy; and my spouse, Pedro Lagos, who was always there to support me.

CONTENTS

Introduction

I've been wanting to write a book since I was in high school. This yearning sprung out of a comment made by my English teacher when she wrote in my autograph book, "You have the writing ability; keep on reading." Since then, these words have been etched in my mind.

I've been procrastinating to write my book until January 2017 when I was diagnosed with breast cancer. This made me think about the wishes on my bucket list, one of which was, of course, writing my book.

What better book to write than my Mom's life story? I've been wanting to write about her life since her passing in February 2010. I was the only daughter of a family of five children. Therefore, I was the only one who had patience enough to listen to her life story.

My mother, Mercedes, had a pen pal from the United States. Her name was Annette Wilhelm and she passed away six months before my Mom did. They had kept writing to each other for forty years. This meeting came about because the Parker Pen Company had put up a stand in the New York World's Fair in April 1964. They were promoting Parker International Penfriend Program where names, ages, and interests were matched to find an overseas penfriend. Annette wrote her first letter to my Mom on 2 August 1964, the start of a lasting friendship that would span over four decades.

My mother had the good fortune of meeting her pen pal when she came to visit us in Manila. Mom also had a chance to visit Annette at her home in Baltimore, Maryland. There, Annette proudly showed her an album containing Mom's letters to her. She had kept them diligently. Unfortunately, my mother wasn't as organized, and Annette's letters disappeared when Mom went to live in the United States and then in Australia.

When my husband and I went to the United States, we also had the good fortune of meeting Annette. From then on, we always received Christmas cards from her. So, we reciprocated this kind gesture. One day, we got a letter from her daughter-in-law Carole, who informed us that Annette had passed away. Annette was ill for the last three years and was being nursed at home by her husband and a health aide. I asked Carole whether she knew of the album of my Mom's letters. She said she had them. Thereupon, I asked her if she could send me those letters. Thankfully, Carole was kind enough to send it to me, and I now have this album in my possession. Unfortunately, this was only one album of the beginning stages of their friendship. I've used these letters in this book to lend more authenticity to my Mom's story. I have filled in the gaps of her life story that her letters didn't cover from my memories and those of others. I am telling the story as if my mother were writing an autobiography.

This book is an insight into the life of Mercedes (Mercy) Marin. Hopefully, her story will instil in your mind that no matter how bad or traumatic your childhood experiences were, you should not dwell on the past but move forward.

Another lesson that I'd like to impart is the importance of friendship. Having a friend with whom we can communicate, even at a distance, and share our experiences is wonderful. because we can express ourselves without reservation and, most of all, have a feeling of being loved for ourselves.

This is Mercy and her story!

Birth

I was born on Thursday April 29, 1920 at home and baptized Mercedes Masungsong in Manila, Philippines. I don't know my weight, length, or the time of birth, since no one, not even my mother, ever talked about it.

When I was one month old, my mother had to leave me in the care of an aunt (Nana Dionang who was completely blind from small pox, which she contracted as a young girl). As a result, my belly button became infected. My mother (Sofia) had just given birth to me and still had to tend to my father (Sulpicio Masungsong), who was very ill, as well as make sure her business was running smoothly. Despite my Mom's efforts and the doctor's visits, my father later died a month after I was born. I know nothing about my father's lineage, since most of his family perished when Taal Volcano erupted in 1911. The only ones who survived were my father and his brother because they happened to be on the other side of the lake, which wasn't affected by the eruption.

My first recollection was when I was about three or four years old. I was in the arms of my maternal grandfather (Lolo Gorio) where we were standing in the middle of a carnival and he was distracting me from my pain as I had one arm on a sling holding up what looked like a splint.

My mother (Sofia) was a couturier and entrepreneur. She owned and managed a fashion shop and catered to the rich and famous. She had seamstresses and embroidery staff in her employ. She remarried one of her embroiderers (Tomas Consul) and had three more children after me. Thankfully, my stepfather was a real father to me and I was the apple of his eye for four years until my stepsister was born. I even bragged to my classmates that I had two fathers, one in the cemetery (Tatay Sulpicio) and Tatay Tomas. They were a bit envious and said I was better than them because I had two fathers and they had one. It was a great life with my new family, and we all lived together in our two-storey paternal home.

My stepfather even protected me from my mother, who was a strict disciplinarian. One day, I did something that, in her opinion, was terrible and deserved a severe punishment. She put me in a Hessian sack, tied it with a knot and left me locked up in an upper room. Unknown to my Mom, my stepfather knocked on our neighbors' door so he can climb through their window to reach the upper bedroom where my mother held me prisoner. He untied the knot and said, "Please, child, you've got to behave from now on; I'm going to get in trouble with your mother for releasing you."

One day, my Mom took me to a large drugstore. Next to the counter, was a section full of ladies who had little black boxes with buttons (typewriters), and they were tapping away and made clicking noises and impressions on a piece of white paper. When I went home, I rolled a piece of paper and started tapping on it. My mother thought I was pretending to play the piano and immediately hired a professor in music to teach me. I didn't like it, as it took me away from my play.

My mother gave birth to two girls and a boy in her second marriage. I loved my new family and I led a happy and uneventful life until I was nine years old. At that time, my mother passed away after a lingering illness.

At my mother's funeral vigil (which took two days and nights), I realized that I was an orphan. It was customary to have a basin in the room for guests, so they didn't have to go to the toilet which was outside the house. The first night, my grandmother ordered me to take away the basin to the back of the house and empty it. I then knew, that I was no longer the pet of the house but a servant. I had no mother and my stepdad wasn't assertive enough to argue with his in-laws.

My stepfather wanted to move out of the house with his children. Of course, he wanted to take me with him, as I was his daughter long before the other children were born. My Lolo Gorio refused his proposal adamantly by saying I wasn't his real daughter, so he had no right to take me away with him. Tatay Tomas, being a quiet and unassuming person, succumbed to my dominant grandfather. Lolo Tomas and I sobbed uncontrollably as we said goodbye. It was the saddest day of my young life.

So, I started a new stage of my life and lived with my grandparents Gregorio and Paula, their daughter Eulalia (Tia Yayang) and her husband Antonio (Tio Tonio) with their son Enrique (Iking) and another uncle, Feliciano (Tio Feli). They were desperately trying to find a wife for Tio Feli, as he was a little crazy due to his contracting meningitis in adulthood. Another person, Teresa, came to live with us, I used to see her with my grandparents when my mother was alive and never really knew about her and just assumed she was my mother's sister. Later, as an adult, I learned that she was my mother's love child before she married my father. Teresa was raised by my grandparents and even adopted their surname. My father and stepfather knew about this secret and accepted it.

From then on, I was treated like an unpaid servant. Sure, they paid my tuition fees to go to school. Schooling was compulsory. Otherwise, they would probably have made me stay home. With all my chores, it was a wonder that I got good grades at school. I thank God for giving me such a good memory. I don't know how I would have managed without this gift.

Childhood & Teenage Years

Everyone knew how my grandparents and my aunt mistreated me. In fact, a well-meaning lady neighbor offered to give me money to run away to go to a convent. I thanked her but didn't accept her offer. I was a voracious reader, and one of the magazines that I used to devour was *True Detective Stories,* in which girls my age were abducted and sold into slavery and prostitution.

Speaking of reading, I was fortunate to have as a friend an African American ex-GI who owned a newspaper/magazine kiosk within walking distance from my place. He rented out his magazines while I sat in the corner of the kiosk, reading. He took pity on me and allowed me to take home magazines to return the next day. I used to read them in the toilet with a lighted candle. My grandmother wondered why I spent so much time in the toilet but was content with my reply that I had a tummy ache when she knocked on the door.

One of our subjects in school was physical education. We had to wear white gym shoes. One day, my gym shoes developed a hole. I complained to my grandmother, but she said I could still wear it. I had to paint the shoes with white polish, including my big toe, which was showing through the hole. Thankfully, our gym teacher didn't notice.

When my Tia Yayang gave birth to my cousin Iking, she suffered terribly because her nipples had no orifices, so she couldn't express her milk. This caused her agonising pain. The doctor advised her not to have any more children and suggested that she drink Shoktong (a Chinese herbal wine/tonic) as a contraceptive. She followed the doctor's advice, and I was her errand girl to go to the corner store to buy this tonic. Our neighbors used to tease me because I was always carrying the bottle of Shoktong many times in the day. My aunt developed an addiction to this tonic and continued drinking it long past her pregnancy age.

When my Tio Feli (the only son of my grandparents) got married, they lived in the parental home where I too lived. His wife, Aunt Isabel (Tia Sabel), wasn't that much older than I was and we became friends. It was a prearranged marriage, and there was no love there, especially on the part of Tia Sabel. They occupied a room on the second floor of the house. When she gave birth to her children at home, I was the maid who had to carry the hot water up and down the stairs. I also had to help her take care of her other children. One day, during one of the episodes of childbirth, my grandmother screamed at me for being too slow in carrying the basin of water upstairs. I was so angry that I retorted, whose fault is it that she's always pregnant! I regretted those words because Tia Sabel was my friend.

My grandfather didn't believe in doctors and dentists. One day, my cheek swelled up because one of my molars was decayed and infected and needed to be extracted. Of course, I was in pain. He gave me one peso and went to work. When he came home for lunch, he asked me how I felt, and I told him it was still painful. He uttered a swear word and said "I already gave you one peso." He probably thought that I was feigning the pain so I could get more money out of him.

When he came back after work, he tied a string around my molar, tied the other end to the doorknob and pulled. The tooth came flying out. Then he pushed a piece of chilli pepper into the hole where the tooth once was, wrapped my mouth with a cloth and tied the knot on top of my head. The next day the bleeding and pain were gone.

Aunt Augusta (Lola Egus) who was my grandparents' other daughter used to visit us on Sunday with her whole family. When lunch was ready, my aunt asked me to tell my grandfather that it was ready. My grandfather used to play checkers with his friends. He was very particular about having a piping hot lunch, so I approached my grandfather, saying that lunch was ready. When he didn't come at my first announcement, my aunts pushed me again to call my grandfather. When I told my grandfather again that lunch was ready, he got up and slapped me across my face in front of his friends. He was a sore loser and he took it out on me.

One day, my Tia Egus came to visit with her husband Uncle Ignacio (Tio Nacho) and their five children in their black shiny Oldsmobile. When they went in, I was so fascinated by this unfamiliar contraption that I brushed my hand over the hood, like one patting the head of a little puppy dog. My grandmother quickly screamed at me not to touch the car. I chided her saying, "You only love my cousins." She retorted, "Yes, I never loved you!" I felt like she stabbed my heart with a knife, but I didn't let on and controlled my tears from rolling down my cheeks. In my mind, I said, "You'll regret this someday!" Sure enough, in her old age, she had to live with me. She used to roll up her mat (she preferred to sleep on our timber floor) every time I got out of bed, even for afternoon naps. I told her not to worry and to continue sleeping. My grandma was like a lost lamb and I know, in my heart, she felt guilty for the way she treated me as a child. Eventually, she asked to live with Teresa, and I said she could if she was happy there. She confessed that she felt out of place when my Spanish-speaking friends used to drop by.

My Tia Sabel was raised by her grandparents, but, unlike me, she was loved, and her grandparents dotted on her. She didn't do any chores or learn how to be a good housewife.

I remember distinctly one incident. It was June 6th, my Tio Feli's birthday, and, since he was the only son, they always celebrated his birthday. With guests and relatives coming, my workload doubled. We didn't have sinks in those days. The tap was so low in the ground that we had to wash the dishes while squatting on the floor. My grandfather was in a bad mood. I was too busy washing up. My Tia Sabel neglected one of the children (as can happen with three young children and a family function going on) and, of course, my grandfather couldn't call her attention about her neglect. So, who got the brunt of his temper? Me! He kicked me so hard that I hit my head on the tap, broke a plate, and cut my finger. My grandfather wanted to continue the punishment. Nobody came to my aid; they wouldn't dare cross my grandfather. With my aching back, sore head, and bleeding finger, I mustered the courage and shouted, "Why don't you just kill me?!" That was like cold water splashed on his face. He left the room but never apologized for his outburst. I've had bouts of vomiting blood from that time because he managed to cut an artery with his kick. I've hated the date June 6th ever since!

I received more physical abuse from my grandfather but learned to take it in stride. My grandmother was no better. She and my Lola Yayang used to fight over my services. My aunt, who lived upstairs, wanted me to help her, and when my grandmother called me downstairs, Lola Yayang practically pushed me down the stairs.

Soon after I learned that Teresa was my stepsister, I had to call her Kaka (which meant eldest sister) out of respect. She would come home from studying with the nuns and was always failing and had to repeat the same grade a few times. Kaka was the favorite granddaughter and kowtowed to them. She would offer to give our grandfather a cup of hot chocolate. She would then go into the kitchen and order me to prepare the hot chocolate, but she brought it to him as if she had prepared it herself.

My mother gave me a silver pen as a present for my high grades. One day, I was trying to reach for something and it fell out of my pocket and rolled behind a big wardrobe. When we had to move, I asked Kaka to get my pen when they took away the wardrobe, as I was busy preparing my nephews and nieces for the move. I never saw the pen again. When my son grew up, he said that he saw one of Kaka's children using the same pen that I had described.

Education

I went through my primary and high school days in a breeze. I was always in section 1 and I had been accelerated twice, so that I skipped year seven and jumped straight to high school.

On the other hand, Kaka wasn't as bright. They sent her to boarding school (La Consolacion College) with the nuns as soon as my mother died. I was young and never questioned it. Later, I realized that they did this because I would have caught up with her because of my acceleration.

Though she lived with the nuns, her clothes still had to be washed and ironed at home. It was my duty to do that, and, once a week, I had to take a bundle of Kaka's clothes to the boarding school. Many times, the road to the school was flooded after a heavy rain. Being a kid, I enjoyed wading through the flood waters.

When my report card came for my senior year, I showed it to Kaka. She, in turn, showed it to the nuns. The nuns were impressed with my grades and offered me a college scholarship consisting of free tuition to obtain a bachelor's degree in Education. The only thing they wanted in return was that I would teach in the same college for two years. I wanted to jump at the opportunity to obtain a college degree but told them that I had to get my grandparents' approval, since they were my guardians.

And, as I expected, they turned me down. They would lose an unpaid servant. I was so disappointed that I must have cried all week.

There was a scholarship grant offered by the Philippine College of Commerce where a select number of students from different schools were chosen. These students, on passing an entrance examination, were eligible to study high school and, at the same time, take subjects that would enable them to obtain a commerce degree upon graduation.

On the day of the examinations, Tia Yayang stopped me from going and said I could go the next day. She needed me to scrub the floor. When I went to the school the following day, my name had been crossed off the list. I was devastated.

I begged the registrar to give me a chance to take the exam. The registrar (Mrs. Marin) kindly explained to me that, although she would like to give me the test, as my report card was exemplary, she couldn't do so because of school policy. Because I was late and didn't turn up on the day of the exam, they couldn't accept my application to take the entrance exam. I cried on the way home and felt like killing my aunt. Although my grandfather chastised Tia Yayang for keeping me away from the entrance exam, the damage had been done.

I managed to graduate from high school with flying colors. I was looking forward to going to university. I asked my grandfather if I was going to enrol in the University of the Philippines, the top university in the country. He said he was sorry, but my Tia Egus borrowed the money he set aside for my education and she hadn't paid him back. I was once again frustrated in my efforts to advance my education.

I bumped into one of my schoolmates who was three years my senior. She told me she was working as a typist and was earning a reasonable wage. I remembered she wasn't so bright at school, yet she had managed to land a job.

So, once again, I approached my grandfather and said I wanted to learn how to type and take shorthand. As an added attraction, the business college I went to offered a Spanish course for free. I had always been interested in learning Spanish ever since I was a kid listening to my mother's affluent clients conversing in Spanish. I would mimic them and think that if I spoke Spanish, I'd be rich too. Come to think of it, my mother was a linguist because she was speaking to her clients in English, Spanish, and French.

My grandmother wouldn't hear of me taking a whole afternoon off from the household chores to study Spanish. But I lied and said it was compulsory. Because of this little white lie, I would land my first job.

Career

When my typing and stenography course finished, I informed my Spanish teacher. He wanted me to stay on, as he said I was his best student. He offered to continue teaching me for free. However, I had a job waiting as the assistant to a kindly old gentleman (Mr. Mencarini) who ran an International Correspondence School. My newly acquired skills came in handy, especially knowing Spanish.

Soon afterwards, Mr. Mencarini retired, but a relative learned about a job vacancy as steno-typist in one of the largest pharmaceutical company in the Philippines (Botica Boie) and suggested that I apply. I asked my stepsister Letty to accompany me. We went there shortly after lunch. While Letty waited in the foyer, the head honcho of the secretarial pool (Miss Carrie) gave me dictation and handed me letters to type. I was there the whole afternoon. When 5 o'clock came, Miss Carrie told me to come back the next day. I had to ask her if that meant I was hired. She laughed and said that I'd get paid for the whole afternoon's work. Letty was so angry with me, as she had to sit waiting for me the whole afternoon. I was so naive that I didn't question why the test for the job took three hours.

I worked as a steno-typist in a typing pool in which Miss Carrie was our supervisor. She was a tough taskmaster but had a kind heart. She quietly talked to me and advised me to tie up my long hair in braids, as it was unprofessional to leave it flowing down my face. One day, I went to work and one of my fingers was swollen because I scaled a fish for dinner. Miss Carrie said that since I was now working in an office, I would have to take care of my hands, as they were important for my job. I was to let my relatives know that I could no longer do chores that would endanger or hurt my fingers.

At this job, I met one of my best friends (Consuelo Grau, pet name Choling). She was a beautiful lady with white complexion and she had Spanish and German ancestry. She spoke in Spanish and refused to speak with me in English, so that I could practice my Spanish. She was kind enough to correct my Spanish, and I was happy for the learning experience. We became friends after she approached me and asked for help with mathematics. She was a clerk in one of the subsidiary companies under Botica Boie and had to compute discounts using percentages but was stumped. I helped her with her dilemma and kept her secret from everyone else.

This was also the time I met Tony Marin (my future husband). Tony was a clerk and worked on the mezzanine floor where he could watch my every move. I never looked up while I worked and never realized there was another floor there. I used to borrow my sister's blouse, and because she had large breasts, I had to put a safety pin on the front of the blouse, so I could use it. Tony started to court me with little notes, romantic quotes, and poems.

Miss Carrie trusted me so much that if someone were absent or ill, I'd take over. One day, one of the telephone operators was ill and Miss Carrie asked me to fill in. After a brief introduction to the telephone system, I took over. However, when all the phones were lighting and buzzing at the same time, I became confused. On one occasion, I pulled out the plug while an executive was talking on the line. I immediately went to the executive suite and sought to apologize to Mr. Smith for cutting his call. After knocking on his door, I went timidly to his office and apologized. Mr. Smith wasn't angry at all, and from that time on, he called me "Pygmy" and asked for me specifically when he wanted work done.

In December 1941, Miss Carrie asked me to be the cashier. The cashier's booth had a solar paneled roof and I could see the American planes flying over to attack the Japanese bomber planes. I was so scared that I lost a check and couldn't balance my accounts. Luckily, Tony noticed my dilemma and wandered to my booth. He helped me find the missing check in the trash bin. After this incident, I allowed him to accompany me home.

I was an office all-rounder. One day, I was a steno-typist; the next I was a telephone operator or a stock clerk. One day, when I was doing the stock clerk work, I caught the flu. I went to work, even though I was feeling very sick. My grandfather was asked to retire from his job as caretaker of the elitist Ayala and Zobel family, who owned San Miguel Brewery, because he had reached retirement age and because business was slow during the Japanese occupation. So, I became the main breadwinner. I couldn't afford not to go to work, no matter how sick I felt. My aunt put some liniment on my forehead with a cross and, because of my high fever, the mark was still obvious.

In those days, we didn't get paid sick leave, until the manager approved it. Miss Carey, our supervisor, seeing my face and how sick I was, recommended my sick leave. However, I needed to balance some stock figures and took the work home.

The next night, Tony passed by my house to pick up the inventory book, which I had finished despite my flu.

In the Philippines (at least in our home) it is customary at around 6 pm when the sun goes down that young people ask the hand of their elders to lay it on their foreheads as a form of blessing. However, Tony came around at about that time, and I neglected to ask for my grandfather's hand. I was seeing Tony to the door when my grandfather called out. When I approached him while Tony hovered at the door, my grandfather slapped me across my face. The pain caused by my grandfather's left hand wasn't as painful as the embarrassment I felt because Tony witnessed the incident. Tony was ashamed too and was sorry because he blamed himself for this punishment. He decided then and there that he was going to take me away from my grandfather and the place where we lived.

Marriage

After the incident as the cashier, Tony began to accompany me home after work. Our relationship blossomed so much so that Tony proposed. Although I had many suitors, I only fell in love with Tony. One of my suitors (Peping) bluntly told me that he was just waiting for me to mature since he had been in love with me since I turned 15. He was so heartbroken that he joined the Army. His father showed me the house that he bought for us, saying this would have been my home if I had married his son.

Since it was the Japanese occupation, my grandfather and my Tio Tonio didn't have a job. My Tia Yayang wanted to take in boarders to help with expenses. This meant I would have had to take care of the boarders' washing, ironing, and most likely help with the cooking. Fortunately, before that happened, Tony and I eloped. It was a public elopement as everyone in the neighborhood was in on it. The only ones who didn't know about this were my grandparents, my aunt and uncle, and Kaka. My stepfather visited us constantly, and each time he left, he carried some of my clothes and shoes. My suitcase was passed from one neighbor's house to the other and one neighbor even offered to lend me money when he learned about our elopement.

We went to live in one of his friend's house after our civil wedding. We married on July 11, 1942 in St. Michael's Church, the same church where my daughter Ginny would later be married in. We wanted a simple wedding and the occupation made it simpler. We all walked to and from the church, and, because it rained hard after the ceremony, we were all wet and cold when we reached home. We had a camera but no film, and we couldn't afford a studio, so we didn't have any pictures of our wedding. Tony celebrated our wedding anniversary on the day of our elopement, but I celebrated it on the day of our wedding at the church.

My aunt conducted a thorough search of my whereabouts with family and friends. When the search for me ended, then we moved in with my in-laws.

My in-laws were very nice, especially my father-in-law Papa Jose. He was pure Spanish bred from Seville and he didn't know Filipino or English. So, I polished the little Spanish I knew with him. He came to the Philippines at 21 as a stowaway in the ship on which his uncle was part of the crew. He recounted that as he was disembarking on the boat when he bumped into a friend (Manuel Villegas) who was returning to Spain. Manuel confided to him that he was returning with a heavy heart because he was leaving the love of his life behind, Amparo Molina. I surmised that Manuel gave her contact details to Papa with a request to take care of her on his behalf. Papa took care of her alright, as she became his wife!

Papa Jose was a darling man. He used to call me his "mascot," as he said I brought him good luck. He used to peddle meat and sausages to his friends and acquaintances. He also had a small fortune, but his wife managed to squander it away along with her own inherited fortune. But they still loved each other and managed to celebrate their golden wedding anniversary. In fact, I organized this celebration at my home.

My mother-in-law was raised by a rich aunt who never had children. Her aunt (Tia Vicenta) was the mistress of the then Mayor of Manila. Amparo inherited a fortune in property when her aunt passed away. However, this fortune was gone when I moved in and nobody really talked about it. Since Amparo was born with a silver spoon in her mouth, she didn't know anything about housework. She welcomed the help I gave. I took over the cooking, cleaning, and washing. However, she asked me to leave the washing of her husband's clothes to her. Papa didn't mind this, as he adored Mama. One day, I washed my father-in-law's shirt and he thanked me, thinking I bought him a new shirt. Mama's routine was to sweep the kitchen floor at 10 pm. One day, I saw her starting to sweep the floor and I told her I already did it at 9 pm. She swept it again anyway. My two brothers-in-law lived with their parents, as they were both bachelors. They were happy I lived with them, as they could now eat home-cooked meals and not the usual takeouts.

One day, it was time for Tony and me to move out to our own home. My father-in-law asked why there was a cart outside the door. When I said we were moving out, his eyes glistened with tears and the cigar in his mouth quivered. He said I was his mascot, but it couldn't be helped. It had to happen sooner or later.

The War Years

The Japanese occupation of the Philippines occurred between 1942 and 1945. We had to abide by the Japanese rules. We had curfew at 9 pm and complete blackout by 10 pm. A Japanese army sniper would shoot at any flicker of light that could be seen from above. No noise was allowed as well. I remember one night, Tony Jr. (who was the baby then) started to cry. We didn't have milk. Luckily, I had a bar of chocolate, fed him that, and, thankfully, he quieted down.

Food, especially rice, our staple food, was scarce. The Chinese cornered the supply of rice, and it was often expensive. Bartering was a common practice. My husband used to buy and sell stuff like tires, spare parts for cars, and anything he could commercialise.

The Japanese soldiers were everywhere, and we had to bow to them every time we ran into them. If we didn't, we would get a bayonet. There were also Filipino guerrillas fighting against the Japanese.

One day, as I was walking, I saw two nuns on the rooftop and, suddenly, shots were fired at a man on the street. The nuns were guerrillas and I saw the man's body running without a head. It seemed that man was a traitor who betrayed his fellow Filipinos.

When the Americans landed and were fast approaching Manila, the Japanese began driving us away from our homes by burning the city down. On our street, they caught a "guerrilla" and, because of this, they were going to annihilate all his neighbors – us! So, they forced us into a straight queue, my stepfather, my stepbrother, my stepsister, my grandmother, my aunt and uncle, and me, ready for execution by gunfire. My grandfather had passed away only a few days before. Incidentally, my youngest stepsister (Lolly) died at age seventeen, a year earlier, with cervical cancer, which was unknown at that time. I'll never forget her dying words: "I don't want to die," but God had other plans for her. She asked to be buried in my wedding dress, and I willingly dressed her in it.

Other neighbors were in the same queue. I was terrified, and I made a vow to the Virgin Mary of Carmel that if our family was spared, I'd wear her brown tunic, which represented her when I went to Church for the rest of my life.

One of the Japanese men who lived in the same street with us (Mr. Tasho who used to own a glass/mirror store called Tasho) was conscripted and made an officer. He was standing near the queue where we were nervously awaiting our turn to be executed. A whole group of our neighbors were shot only 20 minutes earlier. I pleaded with Mr. Tasho to spare our lives. Although we didn't know each other intimately, we grew up in the same neighborhood. He pleaded on our behalf to the highest-ranking officer present there. Then he approached us and said that we could go but had to do it immediately. We thanked him profusely and were starting to move out when one of our neighbors turned back to pick up his hat on the ground. As he bent down, Tasho took out his samurai sword and cut his head off. We all cried out and asked Tasho, "Why did you kill him? He was just picking up his hat." Tasho said, "If I hadn't killed him, as he disobeyed the order to move out, I would have had to kill you all." We hurriedly left this horrific scene and away from our burning homes. We really couldn't mourn the loss of our homes and possessions because we were running for our lives.

The Japanese occupied and ruled the Philippines for almost four years. Then the Americans came to liberate the Philippines. However, the Japanese didn't want to leave any of the spoils of war to them. They again went on a campaign to burn the houses and drive everyone away. This time, my in-laws' place where we also lived also caught fire along with hundreds of homes in Manila being razed to the ground.

Thankfully, the Americans started to build houses, hospitals, and schools and brought peace to our land.

Parenthood

I delivered our son Antonio Jr. in the hospital. Our children were all premature: Tony Jr. – 8 months, 4 lbs; Ginny – 7 months, 3 lbs; Robert – 8 months, 4 lbs; Rene – 7 months, 2 lbs and Joey – 8 months, 6 lbs. Only Joey wasn't placed in an incubator. However, because he was a large baby 6 lbs, and as I had a small uterus, he was pulled out with forceps.

Tony was like any other normal kid, full of life and energy. I made it a rule for the children that after lunch, we all had to lie down for a nap. If we didn't want to sleep, we still had to lie down in bed quietly to rest.

I set the alarm clock for 4:00 pm and put it on top of the children's bureau in their room. This was the cue for everyone to get up. As soon as I nodded off to sleep, Tony would slip out the back way and play with his pals in the street. His siblings were sworn to secrecy. Somehow, he managed to get back before the alarm clock rang. He was popular with his friends and always won any games they used to play whether it be marbles, cards, or hide and seek. How he graduated from high school was beyond me, as he hardly touched his books.

Ginny, on the other hand, was a conscientious student. My husband and I postponed enrolling her in kindergarten thinking that because she was a premature child, she might not cope with school as the other children did. I taught her to write her name in longhand. We enrolled her when she was seven years old. I remember when the principal asked if she could write, she picked up the nun's pen and wrote her name. The nun immediately put her in first grade, skipping kindergarten. As expected, her grade for the first trimester was a whopping 75% average. To console her, her dad said, "Don't worry, darling. When you reach the last grading and you get 90% average, I'll give you 5 pesos." Little dreaming that this would give Ginny an incentive, she got 90% average at the end of the school year. Ever since then, she consistently received a medal in her primary years.

Robert was a quiet, unassuming student. Religion was one of the subjects taught in his school. By the way, because my husband was earning good money, all of our children went to Catholic schools. We were surprised that he got a 100% average in that subject. So much so, that the principal (Brother Paul, a lay priest) offered Robert a college scholarship. The only proviso was that he would enter the seminary to study theology among other subjects. I objected because I said he was too young to oblige him to be a seminarian. If he had the vocation, then he could enter the seminary on his own accord. I regretted that decision. Our family doctor (upon my recommendation) became the school physician. He gladly accepted the scholarship. When his son graduated, he left the seminary.

Rene was a conscientious student. He finished his homework on Friday evenings so that he would have the weekend free. During recess, he used to pick up all the empty bottles in the school grounds and returned them to the canteen. He, of course, received money for his effort. We paid a chauffeur (who owned a jeepney) to fetch our children to and from school. One day the driver complained that Rene was always late when it was time to go home. When we questioned Rene, he said that he had to wait for his pencils and erasers to be returned. He used to rent these out to his classmates. He also sold sheets of writing paper to them. Rene learned to touch type through self-study. This helped him when he joined the U.S. Navy. After graduating from Navy training, the first thing they asked was for anyone who could type. Out of the 300 new recruits, he was the only one who could type. He was immediately promoted to corporal and never swabbed a deck.

Joey was the cheeky one. He was also a good student and a good swimmer. He won medals for his swimming prowess. We didn't own a TV set when we moved into an apartment. We found out that he used to hold onto the window railing in our neighbor's house, so that he could watch TV. We reprimanded him for that because he could fall and hurt himself. My husband, just to console him, said, "Don't worry, son, we'll buy a TV set one day." Joey retorted, "Sure, but when? When I'm old? When I'm dead?" He said this in mixed Spanish and Tagalog. That weekend, Tony bought a second-hand black and white TV.

After lunch, I usually ask one of the kids who took turns daily to pull out my white hair with a tweezer. I asked them to lay the white hair on a black sock. We used to have a terrier dog then. Her name was Beauty and she had white fur. When it was Joey's turn to pull out my white hair, I always wondered why it didn't take him long to take these out compared to his siblings. He would show me the black sock after just a minute and it would be covered with white hair. After so many years, I learned that Joey used to pull out Beauty's hair and lay these on the black sock. He was very resourceful in that way.

I never thought that I would have to care for a baby full time at age 45. But that's how it was with Maria Paz (Maripaz). She was the daughter of my cousin Nita (daughter of Tia Isabel). Nita had two other children and was giving away her unborn child. We could not adopt Maripaz legally, since we already had children of our own. We just asked Nita to sign a paper that she willingly gave us her child, as she was unable to care and support her. She took our surname Marin and we raised her like our own.

Trials & Tribulations

When my husband Tony was promoted to purchasing manager, he received a lot of invitations for lunches and especially dinners and even drinks from the suppliers. I waited for him for so many nights to eat dinner together as a dutiful wife. Because of this, I developed a stomach ulcer. I began to throw up blood and lost a lot of weight. Tony realized how sick I was because I wouldn't drink coffee and I wouldn't read my favorite magazine the Reader's Digest. Tony wasn't a religious man, but he went to the Nazarene Church and walked on his knees to the altar to pray for my recovery. I guess God listened to him because I did recover. I never waited for Tony again to have my lunch or dinner!

An incident that will indelibly be etched in our minds happened when our son Tony was 17. My eldest sister Kaka called me and said her daughter Emily ran away from home. I didn't know what I could do, but, being a dutiful sister (probably more to comfort her), I went to their home with Ginny.

We used to live near a university. A party was going on for the end of the school year celebration. Naturally, as with any celebration, beer and wine were served. It was late one evening and my eldest son Tony Jr., was already sleeping. He was woken up by our housemaid Paulina (who had been with us for thirty-three years and was treated like a member of the family) and Fely (one of my protégés staying with us for her Chemist Government Board Exams). They asked him to wait for us at the corner of the street where we would alight from our trip from my sister's place.

As he waited, a gang of men purportedly professors from the nearby university approached him. They were very drunk and accidentally mistook Tony for a juvenile delinquent (Bobby Lopez) in our neighborhood. That day, Bobby was incarcerated in the municipal jail. One of them brandished a hand gun and bashed my son across the face, breaking his nose. Then they chased him through the streets and threatened to shoot him. My son was running for his life. His face bleeding, he hid under the funeral hearse at the end of the long street. This gang was looking for him while riding a car to kill him.

When Ginny and I arrived, we were shocked to see my son bleeding profusely from his broken nose. The next day, I went to the police station and pressed charges against the professors of this university, especially the fellow who bashed my son with the gun. Someone from the corner store witnessed the incident and was familiar with the names of my son's assailants.

Tony was studying in a Catholic university for a degree in Commerce. He was already in his second year. After this terrible incident, he refused to go back to university. Every time there was a knock on the door, he would run upstairs frightened. We took him to psychiatrists and were told he had a nervous breakdown and developed a persecution complex. He also had violent attacks of temper.

We found out by accident that Tony Jr was having those violent attacks of temper because he was in agony. Bobby Lopez purposely drew a tatoo across his leg without local anesthesia. He just gave him a bottle of wine. He was not aware that Tony Jr was taking tranquilizers and wine was taboo. Because the tattoo was done crudely, the leg became infected and Tony was crying in pain. We heard him sobbing in his room and we went to his aid. To our dismay and horror, we saw his tattooed leg. My husband began to weep. I never saw him weep in all our married life. In those days, only jailbirds had tatooes. Seeing my husband in that state and my son suffering, I screamed "I wish the person who inflicted this on you will die a violent death"!

Right around this time, I was also bleeding internally, and the doctor advised an exploratory operation. In 1972, there were no CAT scans. Therefore, I had to undergo four hours of surgery only to discover that I had a tumour. So, I had a complete hysterectomy. Even while I was at home recuperating from the operation, my son would sometimes come and threaten to stab me in one of his dark moods. But I maintained a brave front and showed I wasn't afraid of him.

In one of these episodes, he threw a shoe at my head. When he threw a punch at Robert's face, we organized his confinement in a private psychiatric hospital. It was a blow to our finances because we took him to a private hospital. In the end we had to put him into a public psychiatric ward, as we spent all our savings on him. Thus started seven years of turmoil and heartache, in and out of mental hospitals and depleting our financial resources.

The doctors advised a change of environment when Tony Jr. came out of the hospital. So, we decided to move out of the suburb we were living in and into another more respectable area. We found a beautiful huge house with a front garden and a large back yard. We moved on a Saturday afternoon and Tony Jr. was going to be discharged from the hospital the next day. After lunch, we decided to take a little nap, as we were all tired from the move.

My mother-in-law was going to live with us, as there was now room for her. She always wanted to live with us as her daughter worked and entrusted her care to the servants. She stayed with her daughter Maria while we moved residence. My brother-in-law Gabriel (Bitoy as we called him) helped us in the move and took the couch. Just as we were about to fall into a deep sleep, a taxi pulled up and my sister-in-law and mother-in-law stepped out of the taxi. Maria was angry that her Mom wouldn't stop nagging her to take her to Mercedes. They had to drag my mother-in-law up a set of steps to the living room. When they reach the top of the stairs, Maria (who had a keen sense of smell) said that she smelled smoke. Bitoy went to investigate and came back running and shouted, "Fire! Fire!" They had to drag Mama down the stairs and into the street. I panicked and shouted, "Move! Move!" Some boxes were still unopened, and we started to pick up our things to save. We dragged the children into the street and asked them to wait and watch our things. One guy offered his trolley to put our blankets and sheets on. I thought he was a good Samaritan. He turned out to be a thief and ran off with what we had salvaged. The firemen came but instead of splashing our house with their hoses, they pointed it toward our Chinese neighbor's house to keep it from catching fire. Apparently, this neighbor paid them money to do just that. Since we were only tenants, we didn't have insurance for our contents and got no money.

Another neighbor kindly offered us to stay with them for the night. We went inside and waited for my husband to pick up Tony from the hospital. Tony was still under medication and the neighbor almost turned him out of her yard because he couldn't talk coherently from the medications he took. Later, my sister Kaka came to pick us up. We went directly to her place with the handful of clothes and things we managed to save. We stayed with her and her family for a month while we looked for another place to live. Kaka offered to go back to the burnt house with Paulina the next day to try to salvage something. Our house burnt down on May 19th and school opened on June 7th. All the uniforms, shoes, and books had been burned. I had to buy these for the children again. My children complained they had to sleep on the floor and weren't happy with the meals. Kaka wasn't a good cook. But I forced them to keep quiet and swallow the food with water, even if they didn't like it.

Another health trial awaited me. I had a small cyst in the corner of my eye and I went to an eye, ear, nose, and throat specialist. Instead of worrying about my eye, he said he wanted to do some tests on my throat. Sure enough, I had polyps in my throat which could be cancerous if not removed.

I hadn't noticed that there was something wrong with my throat. In retrospect, my voice was getting lower and lower. So much so that when one day, when I called Ginny at work and her office mate answered, she jokingly commented to Ginny, "She said she was your mother, but she sounded like your father!"

My In-Laws

I had good relationships with my in-laws: my parents-in-law and my husband's siblings (except for one brother-in-law), and I am grateful for this.

My father-in-law (Papa Jose) was a quiet unassuming man. He loved his wife dearly and never crossed her. My mother-in-law (Mama Amparo) was a jealous type and when she learned that Papa had to pass in front of the house of a previous lady friend, she forbade him to pass that way again. Even if Mama would not see her, he would go around a longer route to visit a customer to obey her wishes. He would sometimes come and visit me at lunchtime as a respite from the heat during one of his rounds, but he didn't stop to eat because Mama was waiting for him for lunch.

One day, I stopped by their house since they lived close to my sister Kaka. I just said hello by the door and noticed his eyes were yellowish. I decided to take him to the doctor. He developed jaundice and the doctor advised that I check him into a hospital for some more tests. We later learned he had problems with his liver. I took him home with me, so I could take care of him and ensure he took his medications. We were living in a huge house then with a front concrete yard and a fruit and flower garden at the back. I used to walk with him around the house, especially on sunny days. Rene was two years old when he lived with us. Rene had a playpen in the corridor leading to the bathroom and he used to lean on the playpen and talk to the baby. He stayed a month until he was feeling alright to go home.

Six months later, he had to be rushed to the hospital complaining of abdominal pains. While he was in the hospital, I visited him one day when he was sleeping. I waited in the corridor for him to wake up. I had a smoker's cough, so Papa must have heard it and shouted to the nurse, "Mi hija, mi hija" (meaning my daughter, my daughter). The nurse peered out the door and only saw me. Naturally, she was expecting a lady with similar features as the patient but saw only me. Papa continued to scream, and, this time, I went into his room. Papa said to the nurse, "Este es mi hija" (this is my daughter). The nurse opened her mouth in amazement and apologized to me. I had to explain to her the circumstances. That afternoon, his real daughter Maria came to visit. He didn't recognize her and she cried. I had to comfort her by saying that he hardly saw her because she was always working. Papa told me he wanted to go home. I assured him that as soon as the doctor said he could go, I would pick him up. However, a week later, he passed away.

My mother-in-law (Mama Amparo) went to live with her daughter when her husband died. She lost her sight because of glaucoma. Even though we lived next door to each other, I offered to take her in, since she was only left in the care of the maid. She sat in our living room while my children and I doted on her. She loved to sing, and I think this was her way of coping with her blindness. Because her knees were stiff from sitting down constantly when she lived with Maria, I had to drag her to the toilet for her shower and daily needs.

After Tony Jr.'s mishap, we had to move out of that apartment. Mama moved back to her daughter. However, Maria had to downsize, since she had only two children living with her. Maria's daughter (Carmen) studied in the same school as Ginny. Ginny passed by their apartment so Carmen and she went to school together. While waiting for Carmen, Mama used to say to Ginny, "I love your Mom, but she can be a wild beast at times." She recalled an incident when Tony Jr. was a kid and having a temper tantrum. I was going to punish him, but Mama interfered. She blurted to Tony Jr. (who was her favorite grandson) that no one could hurt him. This wasn't the first time that she interfered with my disciplining Tony Jr. So, I told her, "Mama, in this house, there can only be one queen. If you want to be queen, go home and be one." I called out to Bitoy and ordered him to take her home. Mama never forgot that. Despite that memory, she still begged Ginny to tell me that she wanted to live with me. Because she was blind, she didn't know that Maria was sitting having breakfast in front of her and what she said was within earshot.

Poor Mama. She was going to have her desire met to live with me. But the fire took that away from her. However, when she became ill, I decided to take her to my home and nurse her." We were living in the apartment that we moved into after the fire. I transformed our dining room into a hospital cubicle and installed curtains for her privacy. I made her lie on an inflated plastic tube (rounded like a lifesaver) to prevent bedsores. The bed had a matted underlay and I installed a basin under the bed, so she could do the necessary without leaving her bed. She eventually passed away in my care. I was happy she got her wish at the end.

Maria (Nena we called her) was the eldest of five siblings and the only daughter. She was widowed at an early age. Her husband (Peping) was her first cousin. He was living in another part of the Philippines and his father remarried and moved away. When Peping came to Manila to study and met Maria, it was love at first sight. They had to ask a special dispensation from the Pope to get married. Because Peping was a road construction engineer, the Japanese seized him and forced him into hard labor to build their roads in a secret place. When they released him, he was a broken man. He never spoke about it, but he retreated within himself. The only thing that kept him from losing his sanity was his love of chess. He developed lung problems, which we assumed came from the torture he received at the hands of the Japanese. Maria then had to work as a salesperson with one of the prestigious jewelry shops in Manila. Her spinster sister-in-law and her maid took care of her five children, the youngest of whom must have been four years old.

Jose Jr. (Pepe) loved music; Caruso and Mario Lanza were his favorites. He was an electrician, which he learned on his own. He also had a pet project, building his "roleta" (spinning wheel), which he wanted to sell to casinos and/or carnivals. However, it never got off the ground because it could be controlled by anyone handling a secret switch. He was still a bachelor at the age of fifty when one of his well-to-do cousins gave him a job as head foreman in a tobacco factory. One widow in his neighborhood, Aling Maria, saw a golden opportunity and latched onto him. However, she was bossy and waited at the door of the factory for him every payday. Pepe was a kind and gentle man and Aling Maria took advantage of it. Mama screamed at her and threw her out of her home when she was going to hit Pepe with her umbrella during one of their rows. It was hilarious because she was fighting battles for her son who was a grown man of fifty!

Jesus (Susing) was a good-hearted man and hardworking. As a teenager, he lived with his sister Maria who was a neighbor of Rosario (Tayo). Many times, Susing would visit her to have a cup of coffee. Maria used to lock her food cupboard when she went to work and would forget to unlock it. So, when Tayo was moving to go to a new home, she didn't have to ask Susing twice if he wanted to live with her. Tayo's children (three daughters) were already going to college and her husband (Andres) was working as an engineer in the City Council. So Tayo wanted some company apart from her long-time maidservant (Andang). Susing landed a good job as a clerk at an import/export shop where he was given a position of trust after a few years. He had a girlfriend, but she became ill and died. He remained a bachelor for quite some time. Andang used to call Susing *señorito* (little master) as a sign of respect. When Tayo and Andres passed away and all the daughters married and moved away, Susing married Andang. Tony and I were the principal sponsors at their wedding. Andang would call Susing Señorito Susing out of habit, and I had to remind her that she didn't have to address him as such, as he was now her husband.

Gabriel (Bitoy) was the youngest. My husband helped him to land a job as a messenger boy in Botica Boie where he worked. Bitoy was the carpenter in the family. However, when I needed his help with this, I had to supervise him. He didn't have the drive or the initiative. Unlike him, Tony worked his way up in that company from messenger to manager. He used to hang around at our place after work and on weekends. When we went to Iloilo, he became lonely and depressed. He took solace in drinking and became an alcoholic. One day, he fell because of drunkenness and cut his eyelid. He took the jeepney and went directly to our place instead of going to her sister's home, which was halfway to our home. I took care of his wound. When he became ill of liver cancer, he asked to live with us after the doctors at the hospital said they could do nothing for him anymore. When he arrived after Tony picked him up, he remarked, "Home to die, Edeng, home to die!" I did the same thing with transforming our dining room as I did with our living room when I nursed Mama. Since I wasn't strong enough to carry Bitoy to the bathroom (all 32 kilos of me!), I had to give him a sponge bath while he was lying in bed. Susing arrived one day while I was cleaning Bitoy's intimate areas. I think then and there, Susing decided that he would marry someone so as not want to burden me when he became ill, as I had taken care of three of his family members on their deathbeds already.

Manuel (Manoling) was the most problematic of my brothers-in-law. He had a fair complexion and was the handsomest of the brothers. I had first seen him when he came to Tony's office in Botica Boie. Tony was promoted to Chief Clerk and had a secretary. His secretary would remark to me, "Here comes Mr. Dineros." I thought that was his name. Later, I found out that Tony's secretary called him that because he only came to see Tony to ask for money. He was still single back then and unemployed.

Somehow, he managed to land a job as an order taker in one of the largest distilleries in the country. He just went from liquor store to liquor store to take inventory of the wines his company offered and take down their orders for restocking. His job involved traveling to other towns and interisland.

In one of these travels, he had to send money through the post office money orders. He was too proud to ask for help in filling out the money order form. So, he took the money with him on the train. It was an overnight train and he couldn't sleep because he was afraid someone might rob him of the large amount of cash he was carrying. On one of his trips, he went to Iloilo City on Panay island (little dreaming that I would live in Iloilo someday). He met a waitress, Adelina, who was helping her sister, the owner of a local café/restaurant. Soon after, they got married and went back home to live in Manila. The first thing he did when they arrived was to resign from his job. Fortunately, Maria managed to get Adelina a job in the jewelry store where she worked. The job didn't last long because Adelina became pregnant. In those days, they didn't employ pregnant women, so she was let go. Then Manoling continued his previous activities, asking for handouts from his brothers (Tony and Susing) and his well-to-do cousins. He had two daughters during the war already, yet he wouldn't go out to find some means of livelihood but depended on his handouts for survival. Tony, on the other hand, would buy and sell anything he could lay his hands on (with no questions asked about their origin). One day, Adelina commented to me sarcastically, "Oh, Tony is selling stolen goods." I countered, "You and Manoling don't want to get your hands dirty, but you're willing enough to eat from the proceeds of these stolen goods!"

When his daughters grew up and needed to go to school, they enrolled them in an elitist Catholic school. My children went to a good Catholic school too but it was a lot cheaper. I suggested to Manoling to enroll his daughters in this same school. But he didn't listen. He was working then as a wine and liquor salesman. However, when tuition fee payments were around the corner, he managed to sweet talk the nuns into postponing payment. Naturally, he could scrape the money by asking from his brothers. The time came when his brothers refused to give him any more money because Manuel never stuck long enough with any job.

The eldest daughter (Rita) and the youngest (Anita) were good students. Lulu (the middle daughter) left school in her second-year high school. The daughters could look at their report cards but not take them home. This was because Manoling promised to pay the nuns as soon as he found another job. Every time they passed the School Cashier's window, they'd stoop to avoid eye contact. They were very embarrassed because they hadn't paid their school fees.

One day, Manoling could no longer afford to pay rent, as he was jobless again. My husband (the good brother and Samaritan) offered to take them in temporarily without asking me first. We were renting an old but rather large house then. Naturally, Manoling grabbed at the opportunity. That temporary arrangement stretched to eleven months. Not only did we give them accommodations but we also had to feed them.

Manoling's activities consisted of waking up in the morning and hogging the bathroom. Once or twice, he left the door open and I watched as he counted the many slaps of water he splashed on his cheek, the same number of times on the left and on the right cheek. Then he would pat his face to dry, ever so gently.

He would have breakfast with his family then proceed to take his daughters to school via public transport.

Then he would do the rounds of his relatives (his nephews now were working) and ask for money. His wife was under the impression that he was working somewhere. Eventually we had to move to a new house as well because the owners wanted to demolish and build a modern house. They probably would have continued to live with us had this timely event not happened.

When we came back from Iloilo, after living with Kaka for one month, we found a place near where my other sister (Letty) lived. My husband (Tony) was made redundant after Botica Boie closed their interstate branches. He managed to land a sales job that only paid on commissions. On one of his good days that he made a big sale and a big commission, we celebrated with three roasted chickens for lunch. We had just finished lunch when Manoling arrived with his plight that they had no food on the table.

We wanted to share our good fortune with Manoling and his family and asked Tony Jr. to take one of the roasted chickens to his house. When we told him that Tony Jr. was on his way there, he turned red and flustered and hurriedly said goodbye. When Tony Jr.

returned, he announced that Manoling's family was just waiting for him to return so they could eat a big fat fried chicken of their own for lunch.

So, we had caught Manoling lying that his family was starving. That incident didn't keep him from making it a daily habit to ask for money. When we moved to a bigger apartment, next to Maria, the unfortunate thing was that Manoling could just walk from his place to ours.

He would routinely get a bag of bread and then proceeded to our place to ask for money. Sometimes, we were still asleep, but he would walk up the stairs to our bedroom and knock on the door. On one of these occasions, we had lady guests from Iloilo sleeping on the same floor, but he still came up and knocked on our bedroom door. Tony reprimanded him for being disrespectful. Do you think he minded that scolding in front of the other guests? Not at all. That's why we called him a face with double-walling; he had no shame!

When we moved into the small apartment after the fire, Manoling still kept on coming and asking for help. One day Tony had to undergo surgery on both hands for carpal tunnel syndrome. When he learned that Tony was in hospital we went straight there. I happened to be asleep on the bed while Tony was in the recovery room. Kaka there too and asked him what he wanted. He remarked I am waiting for Tony. What, didn't you know he is in surgery, it will be a while. What do you want? She knew full well what he wanted. He unabashed told her he needed money for whatever lame excuse. My sister handed him some money and he said "Tony will pay her back." She retorted, "what if he does not wake up?" He was dumbfounded and offered no reply. It's no wonder my sister disliked him.

A former well-to-do classmate of Robert, who was going to Spain for business, wanted to learn some conversational Spanish to see him through the trip. Robert suggested that I teach him. On one of these tutoring trips to his home, I bumped into Manoling. He queried why I hadn't been visiting them. I told him I was giving Spanish lessons. He sarcastically said, "Can anybody now teach?" I know he was always envious of my brains. I countered, "Well, the little I know is a lot for some people!"

One one occasion, when he was again asking for some money, Tony was giving him some advice and he complained, "Please don't argue with me about my situation." I countered, "Your situation – ever since I've known you, you were always in this situation, with or without a job!" He was speechless and hurriedly made excuses to leave.

I might mention that when Manoling was a young man in 1939, he was drafted into the Spanish army. In those days, the only prerequisite to become a Filipino citizen was to vote. He didn't vote and remained a Spanish national. He was on the ship halfway to Spain to fight the Spanish Civil War when it was announced that the war was over and General Francisco Franco was now the new ruler of Spain. So the ship returned to the Philippines and Manoling never arrived in Spain.

When one of his daughters married and moved to Canada, she wanted her parents and siblings to join her. However, she could only sponsor them one by one, since she had three children of her own. But arrogant Manoling went to the Canadian Embassy and demanded that all of them be given visa at the same time. The embassy must have laughed at his face and ignored his demand. I never heard if they were ever granted a visa. Next thing I knew, he got an approval to move to Spain, with the proviso that they never return to the Philippines. You see, he never paid taxes, neither to the Spanish nor the Filipino government. If he returned, he would have to pay back taxes to either of the two governments.

Because he was a Spanish citizen and became a soldier (though short-lived), the Spanish government Social Security Department helped him with free passage to Spain and a government subsided housing. The lucky devil!

What he didn't know was that we were happy he was going, the parasite as he was. He was already making plans to make the rounds with his nephews and nieces (including Ginny) who were now working, to ask for financial help. The last I heard, he died a month after Tony, my husband. In fact, I believe Tony took Manoling with him on his journey to the other side, to rid his family of the burden!

Annette & Mercy

Tony Marin (My husband) & I dancing

My family & I taken in Dec 1967

My adopted daughter Maripaz

My cousin Pedro Masungsong - extreme right

Kakang (my cousin Pedro's step-sister) & I

My in-laws Jose & Amparo on their
50th Wedding Anniversary

Tony's brothers (L-R - Susing, Tony, Manoling & Bitoy)

My sister Kaka & my friend Kay (4th from left)

My niece's (Dolly) Wedding where I was
matron-of-honor & Ginny the bridesmaid
- Jan 29 1967

My Friend Choling & I - April 1989

My friend Teresit & I - taken on Feb 26, 1995

My friend Ester (on my right), then Fely
(Emcy's sister) & Mari (Nena's son)

My friend Rosario (Tayo) & I

Tiyang Nat & Tiyang Loleng from Iloilo

My friend Nita & I

My friend Lucy (seated next to me)

Lilly Marin (grandaughter), Joey (my son), Paulina, Amada, & Editha (Amada's daughter - my helpers)

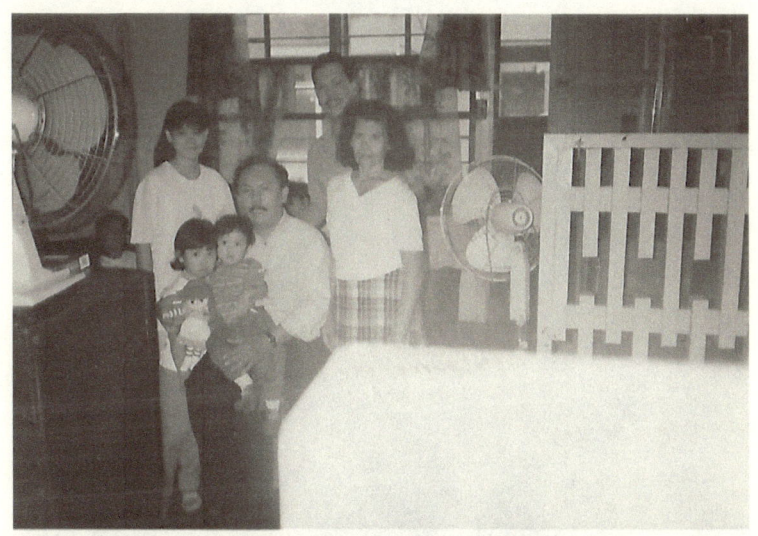

L-R - My granddaughter Lilly with her sons , my
sons Robert & Rene & my helper Paulina

Emcy & I

Emcy with Annette & Gordon Wilhelm July 1966

My Helping Hands

Fortunately, my husband Tony had a good job. He became Purchasing Manager of Botica Boie and was earning enough so I could stay home with the children. We could even afford servants.

My first helping hand was Ingga. She helped me with the cleaning and the laundry. I was always in charge of the cooking. However, she didn't stay very long, a couple of months. Still, I was grateful for her help, as I had just given birth to Ginny. Ingga had to go back to her home town to help her mother.

The next helper was Pilar, my laundry woman. She would pick up our dirty clothes and return them the next day, ironed and all. She also did this work for our neighbors. She was still doing this for me until my second pregnancy. However, she became ill and had to cease heavy work. Pilar visited us often, especially when she needed financial help. I was glad to help, since we had a good income then.

When Robert was born, Pilar visited me at home and had a young lass (around 15 or 16) with her. Her name was Paulina and she was in need of a job. She was an orphan and she came from a southern province called Bicol. There was a fable going around that the women (mothers and/or sisters) from Bicol worked as maids or servants to send their brothers to the seminary. Since I was also in need of help, now with a two-year old child (Ginny) and a newborn baby (Robert), I hired Paulina. She had no formal schooling, so I suggested she enrol and I would pay for it. She refused because she would have had to start in elementary school at her age, and she felt embarrassed. As the saying goes "you can take the horse to water, but you cannot make it drink." I did teach her how to write her name at least. I even invented a birthdate for her.

Paulina lived with us for forty years. When our financial situation was at its lowest (due to Tony Jr.'s illness), I told her to find another employment, as we couldn't pay her anymore. She decided to stay with us for room and board but no pay. Actually, we treated her as family. She even learned how to speak Spanish, a language we spoke at home. When we went to Iloilo City, the plan was for her to go by ship with our two dogs and our furniture. However, she fell ill with the Asian flu and we had to fly by plane and left the dogs behind; one terrier (Lady) with my sister Kaka and the other (her son Tagpi) with my brother Luis. Kaka complained humorously that at her old age she had to learn to speak Spanish to communicate with the dog!

In Iloilo, since we were living on the upper house, the water level didn't reach our taps. A pump in the back yard needed to be pumped to bring water to our house. That's why we needed male help. We hired Pedro and Pepito. Pedro was a jolly person, always singing or humming while doing his chores. He was small in height but strong just the same. Pedro related that he was a landowner, but didn't have enough money to cultivate his land. Thereupon, we called him "Don Pedro." We called people with money, property, or influence as "Don."

Paulina fell in love with one of our male servants (Pepito). She chased after him, gave him money and presents. When she spent her pay, she pinched my children's piggy banks to have money to lavish on Pepito. Pepito used her by all accounts. Unfortunately, Paulina fell pregnant and with our insistence, they were married with Tony and myself as sponsors. When it was time for Paulina to go and live with Pepito, all of us cried, especially the children.

We were astonished that Paulina came back after two weeks of married life. It seems that Pepito dropped her off (or shall I say dumped) in his rented apartment and didn't come back. We told her we had to go back to Manila. She decided to leave Pepito and stay with us.

Soon we were packing to return to Manila. The children and I had to go ahead, as the school term was starting. Tony, on the other hand, had to finish the inventory of his branch and close it down. Paulina stayed behind with Tony and they flew to Manila together. We stayed with my sister Kaka even after Tony and Paulina returned. Since I was also pregnant, I was always feeling so sick to my stomach and was often bedridden. Kaka reminded me about a superstition in our family, that two pregnant women should not stay under one roof. One of the four will die. I didn't give credence to this belief until something happened. Paulina went to hospital but was told she wasn't due yet. Soon after, I gave birth to Joey. He was my biggest baby weighing six pounds, and he had to be removed from my womb with forceps. The week after Joey was born, Tony took Paulina to the hospital. She was supposed to give birth before me. The baby was overdue alright. Unfortunately, he was stillborn because her fallopian tubes choked the baby.

Paulina doted on Joey as if he were her own son. After all, if her baby had lived, he would be the same age as Joey. While living in the apartment (after the fire), I remembered a funny incident. Paulina was washing clothes by hand at the back of the apartment. I was calling her from the living room but not getting a reply. It was just a small apartment and there was no way she couldn't have heard my voice. A concrete fence separated the apartments at the back and providing a small lane where children could gather and play. Joey was playing there with his friends when a small fight erupted. Paulina heard Joey's cry and rushed out of the apartment, soap and all in her hands and wrists. She went to Joey's aid and scolded the boy who was hitting Joey. When she came back with Joey, I remarked, "I was almost hoarse calling you, yet you heard Joey." She smiled with a silly impish grin.

Paulina came to live with Maripaz when I went overseas. When I went to the Philippines with Ginny, we visited her. She wasn't well and was already wearing incontinence pads. She cried when she saw us and we did too. That was the last time we saw her as she passed away a few weeks later. She was like a daughter to me and I felt very sad with her demise.

Patricia also worked for us. She had finished high school and I could entrust her with grocery shopping and other chores that required being able to read and write. She also took the children to the cinema and fetched them from school. However, a better offer came along and she left. After three months, she wanted to come back. She may have been getting better pay, but the treatment she received from her new employers left much to be desired.

By this time, I had young Victoria as my new help. Victoria was an agile and fast worker and smart too! With her, I was able to launch my pastry business. She could help me with mixing the dough, baking, and packing the meringues and other pastries. She also took care of sweeping and mopping the floors and cleaning the bathroom. Paulina, on the other hand, took care of our meals and laundry. I was basking in the glory of two hired help when Victoria's mother came to take her away. She had been promised to someone in marriage (in exchange for something I don't know) and had to make good on this promise. I was devastated, but what could I do?

With Victoria gone, I ceased hiring anyone and it was just Paulina and me.

My Social Life
& My Friends

My social life revolved around events like birthdays, weddings, christenings, and funerals in our immediate family.

My first friend was my cousin Enrique (Iking for short) and we were of the same age. He was the son of my Aunt Eulalia & Uncle Antonio and we lived under the same roof. We laughed and played together, and we also fought often. So much so that my aunt said, "Maybe you are in love with her." He naturally balked at the idea!

Irene was my childhood friend and neighbor. Her father owned a shoe repair shop. I managed to recommend her to work in the same typing pool in Botica Boie where I worked. She became my constant companion, as we walked together to work and back and ate lunch together.

Even though I was practically feeding my grandparents with my hard-earned money, my grandmother never prepared my favorite meals. Irene would comment "Your Grandma cooked your most hated meal again, didn't she?" She knew because she woke me up from my nap and my eyes would be swollen from crying. I skipped lunch altogether on those days.

My other friend was my Aunt Isabel. She was only a few years older than me and I became her confidante. One day, during the christening of one of her children, my grandfather's sister Maria openly criticised her cooking in front of the other relatives. She came to me crying while I was in the kitchen. I advised her to go back immediately and told her what to say. She followed my advice and lashed out, "Look I didn't offer myself to marry Felix. I was forced into it. I was a princess at my home, and everyone knew and accepted that; why couldn't you?" Maria never criticised her openly again.

As mentioned in the Career chapter, I struck a friendship with Consuelo (Choling). During the war years, she used to visit me and spend weekends at our place. I was already married by then to Tony. She broke off with her boyfriend, who was the boss of her sister Charie. As Choling left my place in one of her visits, her ex-boyfriend was passing by in his car and stopped to talk to her. They rekindled their romance and got married shortly after.

I developed friendships in my married years. One of them was Teresita, a neighbor. It so happened that we had babies right about the same time. My Ginny was born in January and her daughter Zenaida in February. She came to say hello and was carrying her baby in her arms. Her baby looked thin and frail and could hardly hold up her head. She told me that the baby had diarrhea. I suspected as much because I had heard the baby crying in the night. I suggested she substitute the milk she was taking with the boiled water from cooking rice only until her stomach settled. Bingo! That did the trick, so much so that she asked me to be the baby's godmother. Since I was going to be the godmother, I earned the right to suggest a change of name for the baby. She wanted to call the baby Yvonne. I suggested she change it because Yvonne sounded like "ibon," which, in our language, means bird. She changed the baby's name to Zenaida with Nenette as her nickname.

Our friendship blossomed so much so that she left her two children in my care while she ran after her husband who was a womanizer. He also loved to gamble and, oftentimes, she would come to me for financial help, as her husband frittered his pay away. Her husband was an officer in the army and, because she was a captain's wife, she had the privilege of taking an army jet to pursue her husband on another island. She even dragged her young baby boy with her. The boy developed a bit of a hearing problem because of the altitude when they rode the jet plane. Again, I became the godmother of her son Oscar. Then she named her youngest son Rene after my own son with the same name.

Kathryn (Kay) Wassmer was another friend. Her husband Louie worked for Tony, my husband. They asked Tony to become their principal sponsor when they got married. Kay even named her only daughter Virginia after my own daughter and her youngest son Robert after my son. Kay was hoping that one of my sons would fall in love with her daughter. However, my children and hers were fond of each other like brothers and sister. My friendship with Kay lasted until she passed away. Kay was responsible for getting Ginny her first job at the APAC head office of Schering Corporation. She recommended Ginny on a temporary basis despite the boss's hesitancy because Ginny was only 17. When the APAC offices moved to Hong Kong, Ginny stayed on, as she was absorbed by the Philippine subsidiary even after Kay got the redundancy.

Another one of my friends with whom I developed a close friendship was Ester. Ester and her family were former neighbors of my brother-in-law Manuel and his family. In one of my visits to my sister-in-law Adelina, Ester popped in, and that's how I met her. We became good friends. However, Adelina resented this and accused me of stealing her friend from her. I know Ester valued our friendship, even though I was very much older than she was, because she asked me to be the godmother of her two sons.

Rosario (or Tayo as she is familiarly known) made me her protégé. Tayo was older than I was, and I followed her sound advice about a lot of things. I, in turn, valued her as a friend and made her my son's (Robert) godmother. The house that burned down was close to her place. I was so looking forward to spending time with her. Circumstances didn't permit it. Regrettably she passed away, leaving an empty space in my heart.

Lucy was a neighbor and I took the role of Tayo. Lucy was an entrepreneur and I met her when she knocked on our door offering something for sale. I couldn't refuse a neighbor. I cannot remember what I bought from her. Nonetheless, this was the start of a beautiful friendship. Her husband was a philanderer and her mother-in-law a pain in the backside. Lucy used to live at the granny flat behind her in-laws' property. She used to come crying to me because of her husband or her mother-in-law. I advised her to buy another piece of land, build a house, and move away from her in-laws. She followed my advice and told me she couldn't be happier.

In 1957, my husband was assigned to be the branch manager of their pharmaceutical firm in the south of the Philippines. My husband went ahead to find accommodations for the family. He found a kindly old spinster (Tiyang Nat) and her widowed sister (Tiyang Loleng) who agreed to rent out the top floor of their house. When my husband left Tiyang Loleng, asked her sister why she agreed to rent out the place to a family with five children. The previous tenant had two children and she was annoyed with them. Tiyang Nat said she herself was perplexed at her decision. It must have been destiny.

We became close friends with them and their immediate family that they entrusted the care of their nieces (Fely and Nene) to us when we returned to Manila. They stayed with us while studying to take the Government Board Exam for Chemists and the other niece Nene was looking for a job. My husband with his connections placed Nene in a job as a Beauty Consultant with Max Factor. I forgot to mention that we lived next door to my sister-in-law Maria (my husband's only sister). She had three sons, and one of them (Tito) married Nene. So not only was Tiyang Nat a friend but eventually she became family as well.

My Hobbies
& Interests

I love to read. I already mentioned this in the chapter about my childhood. I loved to read *Reader's Digest, Coronet, Pageant, Time, Life Magazine,* and any reading material that I could get my hands on.

My grandfather taught me how to smoke. When he retired, to add to the household income, my aunt took on laundry work for the neighbors. I was the laundry woman. However, I had a weak stomach, and, each time I touched a stranger's clothes with their body odor, I began to throw up. That's when my grandfather taught me to smoke so I wouldn't smell the clothes. I picked up the smoking habit and was never able to kick it. However, I tended to light up a cigarette and, after a few puffs, leave it on the ashtray while I did cooking or other chores. So I could truthfully say that I wasn't a chain smoker.

I also loved coffee. I drank every chance I got. It was expresso coffee but so weak and watery that my children used to kid me that the coffee beans were squeezed out of a sock.

I suppose I can still say that I was lucky. Although I was a servant as a child, when I married, I had two servants of my own. I treated them fairly. One of them, Paulina, stayed with the family until her death. Thus, having domestic help, I was able to pursue some interests of mine.

I studied dressmaking and sewed dresses for Ginny. However, it didn't occur to me to buy a mannequin. Poor Ginny had to try on the dresses many times over. I was so proud to make an evening dress for Ginny's office mate for their Christmas dinner. By the way, my Singer sewing machine was a gift from one of the suppliers that were wooing my husband for their company's business.

I also liked baking cakes and pastries and took lessons on how to decorate cakes. When Ginny's friend (and our neighbor) got married, I baked her wedding cake with all the trimmings. This was also a crowning achievement for me.

At Christmas time, with the help of our servants, I managed to bake ham, prepare homemade pickled relish, and cook ham, potato, and cheese omelettes.

I also made Christmas fruit cake and mini meringues. This mini meringue was my own creation because not only were they bite size but they also melted in your mouth. When one of my friends popped in and had a taste of these meringues, she immediately ordered 5 gallons for Christmas presents. She was a Pan Am stewardess and took a gallon on the plane with her. When the pilots tasted it, they wanted more. The word spread, and I was getting orders for this meringue. I was so busy fulfilling these meringue orders that when Christmas Eve came around, my son Robert was furious because we didn't have a lot of food to celebrate Christmas Eve dinner.

I also took up crocheting with my friend Teresita when Ginny and Nenette were babies. I made baby socks, baby blankets, and baby sweaters. Knitting was another hobby I picked up, but I didn't get very far because, with the hot Philippine weather, we really didn't need woollen garments.

I loved watching game shows. My favorite TV game show was called *Darigold Jamboree,* as they had a cash jackpot which increased every week when no one won it. Ginny signed up for this show. However, she developed cold feet and asked me to take her place instead. The spotlights were so glaring that even with my tinted glasses, I still had difficulty in focusing my vision. Leila Benitez, the game show hostess posed three questions. I answered the first two correctly and when the last question came, I answered, "I think it's the Seven Years' War." Leila asked, "Mrs. Marin, do you think or are you sure?" I said, "I am sure." Then she smiled and said, "You are correct." Suddenly, bells, whistles, and loud music sounded. Because the big prize had been won the previous week, I only received 125 pesos for my trouble. This was handed to me by Leila and the Station Manager while a photographer took a photo that was published in the *Manila Times*. My husband was so proud that he bought about a dozen newspapers and distributed these to family and friends. I used the cash prize to buy an electric massager, as I used to have terrible headaches.

When I was taking care of my baby granddaughter Michelle in Virginia, I was getting bored. Michelle was a quiet little baby and didn't need much attention. My daughter-in-law Lay didn't want me to use her oven to bake cakes because electricity was expensive, and she used to do the cooking herself. So, I took up cross stitching. I continued doing this while taking care of Victor in Australia. My favorite was a cross stitch of the Last Supper in silhouette and I believe it is still hanging on Ginny's dining wall. I also whiled away my time with patching (i.e., remnants of clothing that I put together in small rounded patches to make bed spreads). All of my children, especially the boys, liked them because they came in multiples colors.

While living with Ginny in Australia, I had fun cooking for her family. I used to bake pork buns (called Siopao), macaroons, Filipino steamed rice cake (called Palitaw), Filipino sweet flat rice cake, glutinous rice, and toasted mung beans cooked in coconut milk (called Ginataang Munggo) which was Ginny's favorite.

Grandma Years

I never got a chance to take care of my first granddaughter since Evelyn, my daughter-in-law was a stay-at-home Mom. Tony and Evelyn had another daughter and son afterwards. They later moved in closer to her Mom, so I had less interaction with my first grandchildren.

I was pleased that Rene and Lay, who lived in Virginia, asked me to take care of their daughter Michelle. I almost changed my mind about staying because when I just arrived with Emcy (my adopted niece from Iloilo, Fely's sister), dropped me off from New York, my son said I couldn't smoke because their house was made of fibro, a flammable material. Then Lay suggested that maybe I should refrain from speaking in Spanish because now I was in America. I then countered by saying, "What about you? Why are you speaking in Tagalog (our Filipino language); you're now in America, aren't you?" We started off on the wrong foot so much so that I said to Rene, "I didn't ask to come here; you cajoled me to come and take care of your daughter." I don't remember what made me stay, probably for the sake of the baby Michelle.

My husband Tony was to follow me to the United States, since the sponsorship was for the two of us. However, his medical examination showed a shadow in his lungs. The U.S. government postponed his approval until they saw an improvement in his lungs. Rene arranged for the U.S. Navy Hospital to accept Tony when he arrived. With this arrangement, Tony was accepted to come to the United States. However, Tony passed away within six months of my arrival. I wanted to return to Manila while Tony was still in the hospital. Rene (instead of paying for a commercial plane to Manila) requested a Navy jet to take us, but, by then, it was too late. Tony was already in the funeral parlor for his wake.

My children decided that I should go back to the States to make it easier to accept my loss, and, perhaps, taking care of Michelle would distract me from my grief.

Michelle was a good and quiet baby. She hardly gave me any trouble. I was getting bored just reading and watching television. So, I took up cross stitching again. Since Rene lived in a U.S. Navy compound, there was no public transportation. I had to wait till the weekend to go with them in their car to do shopping and attend church.

On rare occasions, we went to visit a distant relative living in Virginia as well. We also visited Lay's sister and her family in New York during the Christmas break. I was hurt not being able to pursue my cooking and baking interests because my son promised that I could do anything I wanted while living with them. I missed puttering in the kitchen as my daughter-in-law Lay practically ordered me to stay out of her kitchen.

I was so happy to spend a weekend with you Annette at your home in Baltimore. My visit with you was one of the highlights of my life in the United States and for that I am grateful. I was pleased to see that you kept all my letters in an album. I was sorry that I wasn't as organized as you were. I was also very impressed with your accomplishments: organist and choir director at Bethany United Church of Christ, voluntary work at Springfield and Northwest Hospitals, and member of the Woodlawn Khoiristers' Klub. In addition, you've traveled to so many places in the world, a real globe trotter, and your marriage to Gordon is solid and lasting!

When Ginny called me and sent an SOS to come to Australia to take care of Victor, her youngest son, I was delighted. She had three children by then and she really needed my help. They had tried to sponsor me to come to Australia after the first baby was born but were unsuccessful. I suppose because my address was in the USA when they reapplied, it was easier to obtain the approval for my sponsorship.

Michelle was already more than one year old when I left the States, but I found a babysitter for her. She was the niece of my only cousin (on my father's side) and she lived in Virginia.

In Sydney, Ginny gave me carte blanche to run her household. I felt important and needed again. Her job and her social activities kept her busy. She joined the International Toastmasters Club and was chapter president of the club. Pedro had his clothing alterations shop within walking distance of their house. Now that they had three children, they managed to gain acceptance for two of the children in a day care center (which was just in the next street where they lived). They applied for this facility the moment the first baby was born but were unsuccessful.

Life in Sydney for me was bliss. I only had to take care of Victor and I could cook and bake to my heart's delight. Since the shops were also walking distance, I could do my shopping as I pushed Victor in the pram. Victor was a delightful baby. He was always smiling. Since the other two boys were in day care, I could pursue my interests, cooking and baking. I had a cake ready every time the boys had a birthday. All of them enjoyed the pastries and sweets that I prepared, not to mention the meals they devoured. I also managed to pick up my cross stitching and patching.

I was happy when Ginny and family moved to a larger house. Larger meant they had a big yard. They had an above-ground swimming pool and I would join the boys when they swam on hot days. Not that I swam, I just waded with an inflated tire.

I remember a funny incident. Ginny couldn't swim one day because of the monthly menace (as she called it). However, she was watching from the sidelines of the pool. I was wading with the inflatable tire around my waist. Suddenly, the tire flipped over, and I fell into the water head first. I thought I would drown. I shouted to Ginny and she picked me up from the side of the pool and started laughing. The pool only reached my waist when I stood up. I didn't go back to the pool again!

Ginny had three large spare bedrooms. The two boys shared a room, one was made into a study room, and closer to the kitchen was a room that Victor and I shared. We slept in the same bed until he was three. One day, when he was three, he suddenly turned around and said, "I'm a big boy now Lola (which meant Grandma in Filipino), I'll sleep in my own bed." I thought he was going to join his brothers. However, he asked for his own bed next to mine.

When the two boys went to school, Pedro or Ginny dropped them off at school. However, in the afternoon, since school finished at 3:30 pm, I picked them up from school. Victor, of course, walked with me. He would often stop and smell the flowers. One day, he was hopping in front of me when I posed the question (which I suppose all grandparents ask), "How much do you love your grandma?" He turned around and exclaimed, "Higher than heaven..." He paused and continued, "But not when you hit me with a stick!" I used to discipline the boys, but with just a sliver of a Filipino broom made from thin midribs of palm leaves and not a stick. It was a spontaneous response but, nonetheless, effective. I don't think I hit him again!

On Saturdays, Pedro used to work half days. Ginny and I took turns taking the two boys to violin and piano lessons, which were two and three blocks from the house. Naturally, Victor, who was around four at that time, tagged along. One Saturday, while waiting for the piano lessons to end, I sat down on the bench across the street and Victor climbed the small tree next to it. One gentleman approached me and invited me to go out with him to the club. I replied, "I'm sorry but I'm waiting for my husband." Perched on the tree, Victor shouted, "But I thought you said your husband was dead!" Fortunately, the man took the hint and walked off. I was so embarrassed.

Pedro and Ginny decided to subdivide the property. They built a new house at the back (doing away with the swimming pool) and sold the house in the front. However, when they applied to the Local Council, they postponed building the new house. They first went to Chile to promote their Amway business. The two eldest boys, Anthony and Richie, went with them. I went with Victor to the Philippines. Pedro's brother minded the house and his business.

When Victor and I went to the Philippines, he was eight years old. It was a bit of a culture shock for him. The weather was hot and humid, there wasn't enough water, and the traffic congestions and flashy jeepneys were all new to him.

He looked for the flush in the toilet, but, because there wasn't enough water or pressure, we had to drop a bucket of water into the toilet bowl. In the jeep that Tony was driving, he looked for the seatbelt, which wasn't compulsory in the Philippines. He did enjoy the attention of our relatives, who pampered him. We celebrated his 9th birthday with a huge birthday cake shaped like a carousel. This was unlike the cake that I usually make for his birthday and it was one of the highlights of his visit to the Philippines.

Ginny came back to Sydney with the two boys and I did too because school was starting. Then Ginny went back to Chile to help Pedro with expanding their Amway business.

One unpleasant incident happened when I was in charge of the children. One day, I wasn't feeling very well, so I asked Anthony and Richie to walk to the nearest grocery store to buy some essential foodstuff. However, this meant that they had to cross a busy street. Anthony decided to jaywalk in the middle of the road instead of using the pedestrian crossing. Richie refused to cross the street with Anthony and witnessed Anthony reeling through the air as he was hit by a car. Fortunately, Anthony fell on the sidewalk and not on the street with the ongoing traffic.

The police dropped off Richie at home and, to my shock and horror, informed me that Anthony was in the hospital. I couldn't rush to the hospital with the two boys, so I called Pedro & Ginny's upline who happened to be a dentist. He went to the hospital and I was relieved to hear that Anthony had a concussion but no broken bones. He also called Pedro & Ginny in Chile.

When Ginny came back from Chile with the boys, she received a notice from the Local Council that they had only three months to present the plans for the new house or the development application approval would expire. Ginny sought the first architect she could find and approved the drawings he drafted to meet the deadline.

The plans specified four bedrooms. One master bedroom and three bedrooms for the boys. Victor was still joining me in one of the bedrooms. They purposely put a sliding door that led to the backyard, so I could smoke outside.

However, by the time the house was built, the boys had grown up. It would have been awkward to share a room with Victor because he was now a teenager. So, I decided to move out. Thankfully, a social worker helped me find a retirement village that I could afford with my pension. This was a motel converted into a retirement home; therefore, the apartments were tiny.

After I moved in and Ginny and family left, I sat down on the sofa and started to cry. I had been so happy living with Ginny and her family. But I had to accept the change of circumstance. Other seniors lived in the village, and I was soon making friends. Ginny also dropped by whenever she could for a visit and always brought the children with her or just Victor.

I wasn't altogether happy in this retirement place because I had to walk through a secluded dirt road to enter the premises. I felt lonely and abandoned. Also, it was located behind a hospice, which was kind of ominous.

Fortunately, my application for social housing was approved thanks to the same social worker. I was ecstatic to learn that the new retirement village was a stone's throw from Ginny's home and I could walk to visit them. It was also like a little studio unit, but it had all the facilities (e.g., living/dining room, kitchen with a fridge and stove, a spacious bedroom and bathroom/laundry with a built-in washing machine and dryer). I became friends with two other elderly ladies, and one neighbor and I shared stories while we both smoked our cigarettes. There was a shared clothing line and a little garden including parking space for those who could still drive and for the visitors' use.

I didn't have an opportunity to watch my two granddaughters' (Joelle nicknamed Champy; and Jacqueline nicknamed Jackie) from Joey's family grow. They moved far away from me. I would only see them when they invited Pedro & Ginny for their christening and their first Holy Communion. Well, at least they made Ginny one of the godmothers of Champy. I guess Belle, my daughter-in-law, harbored a resentment toward me. When they were still in the courtship stage, I wasn't in favor of her practically chasing my son. Call me old-fashioned and raised by traditional grandparents, but I couldn't change my principles.

Twilight Years

Dear Annette,

I miss your letters. Why haven't you written? I may not be able to write you as often. I am going back to Manila because Ginny and Joey think I can no longer take care of myself. The plan is I am going to live with Maripaz. She however lives about two hours away from Manila, up near Mount Makiling and where the University of the Philippines Agricultural College is located.

My children came to this decision to send me back because I've been forgetful lately. I've been misplacing my house keys as well as forgetting to eat my meals. One day, I forgot to say goodbye to Ginny when I left her home, and they came looking for me. They thought I was lost. Last week I went out of my apartment to buy a packet of cigarettes. I woke up in an ambulance. They said I slipped and bumped my head on the curb. It seemed I had a concussion and hurt my arm in the fall. Luckily, I only spent one night in the hospital and they discharged me.

In Manila, Maripaz picked me up at the airport and I stayed at her place for a week. As you know, Maripaz has a health issue with her collapsed lungs. In addition, she has three children (two boys and one girl) who were all students and there wasn't much room in her house for me to stay there indefinitely. Her husband you know lives in Japan and visits them three times a year. Maripaz cannot travel on a plane because of her condition.

My children agreed that I should stay with Tony and Evelyn in Quiapo, Manila. As you know they have a family business of selling cooked chicken in a portable kiosk by the sidewalk. They live in a three-storey house and it meant going up and down those steps, even going to the bathroom. One night I almost slipped down the stairs. Were it not for the quick response of one of the young men who worked for them, I would have had a terrible mishap.

Then and there, Evelyn called Ginny and decided she would hand over the business to her eldest daughter who was part of the business anyway and move to Santa Maria, Bulacan (where she inherited the land from her Mom and built a small house with room enough for us to live). It was comfortable enough and there were no stairs to climb. Evelyn also gave up her part-time job sewing as a dressmaker at home.

Ginny, Joey, and Rene promised to support me and Evelyn in lieu of her giving up her livelihood. I only lived in Quiapo for a month before we moved to Bulacan. I liked their small garden where I could go out and have a smoke. Evelyn lived next door to her sister May, and she used to come and have a chat which I enjoyed. However, all I did was watch television and chat with Evelyn and May. I had no magazines, books, or newspapers to read, as they weren't fond of reading. As far as mental stimulation, I had none, so I was bored stiff.

My cough is getting worse and they've had to rush me to the hospital because I could hardly breathe. It seems I have emphysema, the same ailment that Tony (my husband had). Of course, I knew this was from my smoking. Upon my discharge, the doctor forbade me to smoke. This time, I followed the doctor's advice. Even though I stopped smoking, I'm feeling weak and becoming bedridden. I'm developing a large bed sore because of lying down too much. My legs are also becoming weaker. Evelyn has to practically drag me to the table for meals or to the bathroom to relief myself or for taking a shower. I'm also losing my appetite. I don't know what's happening to me.

This may be my last letter to you. I have lapses of memory and, sometimes, I forget things. The one thing I hope I won't forget is you. I thank you for our lasting friendship. I know I'm going to take this memory with me in the next life. This isn't goodbye, Annette, but adieu. See you in our next life!

Love,
Mercy

Mrs Wilhelm's registration in the
Parker Int'l Penfriend Program

Aug 25 1964

Dear Annette,

I am glad we can call each other by our first names. It gives that feeling of really being friends, don't you think so?

Thank you for your solicitude about my illness. The family doctor came to see me thrice. We have heard of John Hopkins. It is very famous. Many rich Filipinos go there or the Mayo Clinic for their operations.

I see that you have two more years of high school than we do. We have also six years of elementary schools, and four years of high school. Before the war as in my case, we had the seventh grade which was abolished after the liberation. However the Dept. of Education is planning to restore the seventh grade. Some private schools have already done so.

In my time only English was

Sept 14 1964 - Page 1

high. That's why our Church requires us to have our children baptized and confirmed at an early age. Children in Catholic schools are prepared for Holy Communion by the school. I used to teach children from public schools.

If you don't mind please send us a picture (family picture) and I will send you ours as soon as we have one taken. We have not gotten around having our picture taken since our house was burned last year.

Good-bye for now and regards to you all.

Sincerely,
Mercy

taught to us. We were prohibited from speaking any language except English on the school premises. Incidentally, my high school principal was an American, Mrs. Sarah M. England.

After our independence, Tagalog (our national language - chosen among many) was included in the curriculum. Spanish is also taken up in private high schools (3rd & 4th years). However in college it is obligatory for both private and public colleges. My children have the advantage of knowing how to speak Spanish as we speak it at home. Did your Robert study Spanish in high school?

Your Sunday School is similar to our Catechism classes. Only we teach them earlier to prepare them for their first Communion which is usually at the age of

Sept 14 1964 - Pages 2 & 3

October 10, 1964

Dear Annette,

The family insisted that I wait for the pictures to be developed before I wrote you. We borrowed my niece's camera & had these taken. It is good my sister & cousin came to take me to visit an aunt & we had one taken too. I hope you don't mind these pictures all at once.

We have had a good life also despite the trials & tribulations we have been through. We have not done any traveling, partly because we have no car and we have no weekend vacations. Sundays we spend mostly at home. There are so many beautiful places that can be visited in our country that I hope you will come to the Philippines one day. And remember you are all most welcome to visit us. When you come, choose the months from January to June which ...

Oct 10 1964 - Page 1

Our other season, the rainy season, begins on July. The Philippines is composed of so many islands (7,083) that it is not advisable to travel during the rainy season when there are so many typhoons.

All of us dream of going to America one day. Last May Robert participated in the Soapbox Derby. We were all praying he would win. Had he won, he would have gone to Akron, Ohio. Most likely, I would have accompanied him because he is very shy.

My husband and I met when I worked as a stenographer in a drug firm where he was a clerk. We were married during the occupation. After the war, my husband worked again for the same firm as purchasing agent until he was assigned branch manager in the ...

company decided to close of its branches and we came back to Manila, jobless. After six months he was offered a job as sales manager. He handles local & indent sales of four lines.

My children are all premature. Tony Jr - 8 months, 4 lbs.; Ginny 6.7 months - 3 lbs.; Robert 8 months, 4 lbs.; Rene 7 months - 2 lbs.; & Jay, 8 months - 6 lbs. Only Joe was not placed in an incubator.

I must stop now. You must be bored with my family history.

Kind regards to all of you and thank you for your invitation.

Sincerely,
Nancy

Oct 10 1964 - Pages 2 & 3

November 11

Dear Annette,

Are you alright? Mr. Wilhelm and Robert too? You have not replied to my letter of October 10 that I've been wondering if one of you has been ill. If it has been so, I do hope it was not anything serious and you are all well now.

About the snapshots I sent you, will you like me now that you have seen my likeness?

Please send me a picture of you and your family and if possible one of your twin sister, too.

Tell me please, is Dudley Lane a suburb of Baltimore? And what does 21207 after Maryland stand for? We saw a picture of the rib-roofed Civic Center _____ _____ in _____

tion of "Time" magazine and all of us have made a guess as to the proximity of Dudley Lane to this building. Ever since we became pen-friends, anything about Baltimore interests us very much because you live there. It must be a beautiful place.

Kind regards to you and your family, and write to me soon. I enjoy your letters very much.

Yours sincerely,
Nancy

Nov 11 1964 - Pages 1 & 2

Dec. 7, 1964

Dear Annette,

I am glad to hear that everybody is fine.

I did not know that you are doing office work. Business must be good as this is one of the coldest season in years according to the newspapers. We are feeling the cold here too. Last week our weather went down to 20°C. For us, it is very cold already. Has it begun to snow in your state? Do you take your shorthand notes in the Gregg or Pitman system? I used the Gregg when I was working.

Thank you for the picture. Robert and Carole are both good-looking. Is Carole's college near Norfolk? Our dear Gen. Douglas MacArthur is buried there.

Thanksgiving Day is also an official holiday here. But we have

Dec 7 1964 - Page 1

family reunion on my mother-in-law's birthday. Before the fire, she lived with us so the celebration was in our home. Now she is with my sister-in-law as our apartment is very small. She is 82 years old. Poor dear, she is like a child already.

I can't recall now if I've told you that we are all avid readers. Before the fire we had subscriptions of many magazines such as the: Time, Look, Life, Redbook, Coronet, Reader's Digest and Philippine magazines. Right now we have only the Digest subscription & the Time. But a very good friend of mine lends me her old magazines including the Woman's Home Journal & McCall's. Prices of good reading material have become prohibitive for average earners. I had also a collection of pocketbooks by Faith Baldwin and Kathleen Norris. Their books

cannot be found anymore. If there are some, they are cloth-bound and cost so much. What magazines do you usually read?

Mandaluyong is a suburb of Manila. It is almost 7 miles from the heart of Manila which is Quiapo. We have chosen this place because the three younger boys attend the Don Bosco Technical Institute which is very near.

I have enclosed some Philippine scenes with descriptions.

We are wishing you all a Happy Holiday Season and lots of good luck.

Love,
Mercy

P.S. - Please never think you are boring me. Friends do not bore each other. Don't you think so, too? Don't forget your pictures.

Dec 7 1964 - Pages 2 & 3

Dear Annette,

This morning I received your letter and was very much surprised that you did not receive my letter. In fact it was a thank you short letter for the lovely pewter plate and christmas card you sent us. If you have not received it by now I want you to know that we appreciate very much your sending them and the pictures too. Thank you very much. I will ask my husband about the loss since he mailed it for me. He has been in the south for a week on a business trip.

I'm awfully sorry I have not written you in answer to your letter of January 2nd. Shortly after New Year I fell ill and had to stay in bed. I am much better now although I am still under treatment for an internal goiter. I pray I will not have to be operated on as I am very scared as I have heard that goiter operation is performed while one is awake. Two years ago I underwent a major one — a complete hysterectomy. Although I have gained weight (& weigh 96 lbs. now) I have not received my strength.

Even if it is a little bit late I am wishing you and your twin sister a belated Happy Birthday. You are the first I have known to be born on Christmas Day. And still have your mother. Lucky you! My mother died when I was nine & I lived with my maternal grandparents but even they have long been gone.

Right now I am looking at the pictures again. Your son looks like a younger brother of both of you. I like the post card you sent me. It helps me to learn more of Baltimore. Do send me more when you can. I will appreciate it very much.

Speaking of music, to me the most is organ and accordion music. I like to hear it very much. When my mother was alive I had piano lessons but that was a long time ago that now I can play only simple songs with one hand. On Christmas my husband gave Ginny a workable toy organ, Japanese made, with fourteen notes. I play it and the children sing songs with me. I have a horrible voice but I love to sing. My husband, Jr. & Ginny play the ukulele by ear. When we can afford it, we would like an accordion as it is an orchestra by itself and does not occupy space.

Yes Annette, everyone of our churches has an organ. In Las Piñas, a small town of Rizal province, there is the famous bamboo organ built by a Spanish priest, Fr. Diego Cera in 1821. When you come to the Philippines, we will take you there.

When I feel very depressed and troubled, organ music comforts me & I feel nearer to God. Do you feel the same?

We are all very much worried about the Vietnam situation here in the east. We are hoping and praying that the war over there would end already. We have passed through a lot during the Japanese occupation that the thought of another war brings nightmares to us. Please help us pray for peace in our lands.

I am enclosing a picture of the Ifugao rice terraces I mentioned in another letter. They were built by hand centuries ago by primitive Ifugaos. Also a picture of our Legislative building. The building with a tower is the Manila City Hall. The jeepneys you see in the foreground are our mode of transportation aside from the buses. Very convenient for short distances.

I will stop now as I have to go and stay awhile with my aunt. Last year her husband and only child died within forty days. She was with me the last two months. She is with my sister now but my sister has an engagement to attend so I will take Ginny along to see her. When she is left alone she becomes hysterical.

Good-bye for now Annette. Hope you will forgive me for not writing sooner. Best regards to all of you.

Love,
Mary

Feb 16 1965 - Pages 1 & 2

Feb 16 1965 - Pages 3 & 4

March 17 1965

Dear Annette,

Thank you so much for the card you sent me. It has cheered me up very much knowing someone from the other side of the world thinks of my well-being.

I am glad you sent another copy of your picture with Mr. Wilhelm. I carry the last one with me, and the other is in the album. I show your picture to my relatives and friends when I go visiting. You know I have a special album for the cards and pictures you send me.

I can't recall now if I've told you that last Christmas we did not have any gifts among ourselves because we invested in buying a car. It's a 1959 Bel-Air (Chevy). How we enjoy outing nowadays. The children especially are very happy about it. Before, the only places they went out to were the school, the church and of course family gatherings. On the latter occasion, we had to ride in two taxis when we brought our

helper along. Speaking of our helper, she has been with us for the past fifteen years. She is like one of the family, and we actually treat her as one.

Last Sunday, we went to Bulacan, my mother's home province. We visited my aunt who is blind. You'll be surprised to know that the last time I went there was way back in 1952 when an uncle died. And it is only an hour and a half journey. It is because we didn't have a car and to travel comfortably by bus with the whole family is next to impossible. By the way, a province here is like a state in your country although in point of progress provinces are very far behind Manila.

Although it was too late to have sent a birthday greeting to your son, we were thinking of him and sincerely wishing him a happy birthday and good luck all the days of his life on March 13. Did you have a big celebration?

March 17 1965 - Pages 1 & 2

114

Do any of you drink beer? According to many of our friends from abroad, our San Miguel beer rates among the best.

I am glad you liked the place mats. I think the carabao heads are made of acacia. I sent them to let you know I was thinking of you even if I could not write.

Speaking of weddings, here they are dictated by custom or superstition. Those of the Spanish custom prefer the month of May, our month of fruit and flowers. The younger generation prefer to be married in June. Let me tell you of one that was dictated by the full moon. Everything had been arranged already; the invitations sent out. A great aunt consulted her almanac and found out that

---

July 22 1965 - Pages 1 & 2

July 22, 1965

Dear Annette,

I am so sorry I was not able to write you for so long but I am sure you'll understand when you read how it came about.

On Good Friday the youngest had chicken pox. One after the other, the children got it except the oldest. Just as they were better they had the mumps. Then Joey again with the whooping cough. They had to take special examinations. Thank God they are all well now and back in school.

In one of your letters you asked if we have 7 Up and Coca-Cola. Yes, we have bottling companies or rather factories for Coca-Cola, Pepsi, 7 Up, Canada Dry and others. We have also many ice-cream plants.

---

wedding date did not coincide with the full moon. The wedding was postponed and to this day, any misfortune that has befallen that couple is blamed on the postponement. Some think that poverty descends on couples not married during a full moon.

I have the postcards you sent of Loch Haven Dam and the Washington Monument. It must be very restful to promenade in your downtown Baltimore. So different from our downtown Manila. So many people and vehicles - all in a hurry. I love the pictures you send me.

Enclosed are pictures of our famous bamboo organ and our national flower, the sampaguita. The organ was built by a Spanish Catholic priest, Father

---

Diego era in 1821. Except for some minor repairs it has endured until now. When you come, I'll take you there so you can play it. The sampaguita is really as you see it on the picture. It is a bush actually. We string them for garlands and leis. They bloom mostly during the months of April, May & June. Its scent is so sweet. What is your state flower? I read somewhere that every state in your country has its own.

Ginny is working as a steno-typist for the Schering Corporation, Ion East division. It is only temporary as somebody there took a maternity leave. She is continuing her studies at night. I'll write you more about the family in my next letter.

Regards to you all.

Love,
Nieves

July 22 1965 - Pages 3 & 4

115

September 7

Dear Annette,

On my husband's birthday last August 22nd, I showed our relatives and friends the latest postcards you sent me and they were all aghast as we were about the beauty of your Chesapeake Bay Bridge. It is remarkable indeed.

For that occasion I prepared Chinese dishes, native pickles and custard for dessert. Do you like Chinese dishes? They're very delectable.

Were you able to go boat-riding that Sunday? My husband and I had gone once with friends and we enjoyed it very much although I was a bit scared because I can't swim. Do you swim?

Yes once in a while live stage shows are presented through the Theater Guild but not often. I have gone only once and it was a Spanish play. The piece "Hello Dolly" is very popular now. All my children sing it.

Indeed it is very coincidental that your sister got a Filipina for her pen-pal. Is she also from Luzon?

I am kept busy these days filling orders of native pickles and studying dressmaking. My friends like the way I prepare the pickles and induced me to sell some of them. In a month I had three big orders for fiestas. Binny is the one who pushed me to take up dressmaking. Ever since she was a small girl I used to sew some of her dresses, but she has to stay around to try it on for every seam I make. You know, the trial and error method. I

Sept 9 1965 - Pages 1 & 2

One of my nieces is going to Canada by next month. She is a nurse. We are all so excited about it. She is dizzy with preparations and all kinds of advice from relatives and friends. Everybody wants to be sent something from Canada.

I am enclosing three postcards of the same street, Roxas Boulevard. It used to be named Dewey Boulevard; to me and my contemporaries it will forever be. The statue on the Luneta Park is of our national hero, Dr. Jose Rizal, the great Malayan. Did you ever hear of him? He was shot to death on the very spot where his statue stands on December 30, '96, by the Spaniards. He was a linguist, doctor of medicine, law & philosophy, sculptor, painter but above all he loved his country so much he died for it. The building on the left of

should have taken it up long ago but everytime I was ready a new baby came along.

Jenny was given another three month contract which will expire in November. Her office's main is in Bloomfield, New Jersey. Is it near Maryland? Robert passed the examination for inclusion in the model platoon of the school's military training. Do the high schools in your country require military training? Rene decided to be a Boy Scout. I am glad because it may make him stop sucking the bottle. We can't take his milk from the glass. The doctor doesn't advocate forcing him to stop as he becomes nervous. I think sucking his milk relaxes him. He is in the fifth grade already!

Sept 9 1965 - Pages 3 & 4

116

Nov 25 1965

Dear Annette,

Thank you so much for the brochure you sent me. I am planning to use it in helping my boys in their studies. Their school requires American textbooks.

We were sorry to hear about the illness of Mr. Wilhelm and your mother's accident. We hope they are both well now. I have been quite ill too so I could not write you sooner, but I am very much better now.

Ginny is now permanently employed by Essex Asia, an affiliate company of the Schering Corporation in Bloomfield, New Jersey. Have you seen the Schering building?

No, we do not have turnpikes. In fact our first highway was opened by the U.S. army after our liberation. Our government is gradually widening it and have built superhighways to the north and south of Manila.

My niece, Emmy Jalero, will fly to Canada by mid-January. She will take up nursing at the Ontario General Hospital. Is it near Maryland?

We are quite far from the eruption although we felt the quakes. It is the first time we learned that our land has 100 volcanoes, 21 of which are active. It may account for the fact that my country is comprised of more than 7,000 islands.

I am so thankful that Tony (my husband) did not take that plane bound for Legaspi. He was scheduled to take that flight but he changed his mind and flew one day earlier. Our airports (domestic and international flights) are quite near us. Passing through the highway it is a 40 minute ride from our place.

My brother-in-law Bert, the husband of my sister Tresa had a stroke last October the 14th. We thought he was going to die as he was unconscious most of the time. Thank God, he is home now although half his body is paralyzed. He is a changed man. My sister met him through me because his sister and I were classmates. He has always been very kind to me that I feel very sad at the fate that has befallen him.

As you may have read somewhere, we have elected a new president come 1966. Enclosed is a picture of our first family.

Ferdinand Marcos is really very pretty. We are all hoping that under this new administration, times will be better.

Last week, on the death anniversary of President Kennedy we watched on television the laying of wreaths on his grave and a commentary on the White House. It is a beautiful place. Have you gone on a tour there?

I almost forgot to mention that my husband sends his thanks for your birthday greetings to him. My birthday is on April 29.

My best regards to you and your family.

Love,
Mary

Nov 25 1965 - Pages 1 & 2

Nov 25 1965 - Pages 3 & 4

117

Dear Annette,

Thank you so much for the Xmas and Valentine handkerchiefs you sent me. They are very nice and I like them very much. I received both on the same day, Feb. 20th. You know, our postal service leaves much to be desired.

Have you received my package? I sent it last November yet. The shopping bag is made of abaca fibers, the blouse is of silk and pineapple fiber, and the fan is a leaf of our anahaw tree. Did you like the records? "Maligayang Pasko aking Hirang" is a Christmas song which means "Merry Christmas my darling." I sent you "A Million Thanks" because it was composed by

you will like them.

I hope you are all well. Is your mother alright now?

Do you remember I wrote you about my niece who was going to Canada? She changed her mind and have gone to Cleveland Ohio instead. She is there now at Sunny Acres Hospital, Richmond Street.

Jinny has stopped her night classes on the advice of our doctor. She became very thin that I became alarmed. My husband wanted her to quit her job but she wanted to go on working as it is hard to find jobs. She had a raise already.

A cousin has left us her baby to be adopted. Last Sunday she was baptized in our parish church with Jinny as the godmother. I baked two cakes and with a gallon of ice-cream & some biscuits we celebrated the occasion. We have named the baby Maria Paz.

Did you see the movie "Sound of Music"? My husband and the children saw it twice and they liked it very much. It was shown in one of our theaters for nine months. Now they are showing "Mary Poppins."

Please extend my kind regards to your family and to you my love.

Happy Easter!

Love,
Jinny

May 10, 1966

Dear Annette,

It was sweet of you to remember me even on your vacation. Thank you very much.

Your country is truly a beautiful one. Have you been to all the states? My niece in Cleveland has nothing but praise for your country's beauty, progress and bigness.

It is vacation time for my children. They passed - although Robert has to attend the summer class for Geometry. At least I'm free from home works for two months. How about your Robert? Is he graduating this year?

I am sure you still remember the eruption of Taal volcano last year. Its surround-ings have been evacuated again because of a possible worse eruption. It is feared that the big crater will be the one to erupt this time. We pray it will not as the province has not recovered yet from the last eruption.

When my niece flew to Cleveland, I planned on send-ing you a sampaguita bush and some mangoes, but we heard that they will not be accepted on U.S. customs. The bush has flowers already. I am happy about it as almost everything I plant die, but this one which I planted for you has flourished.

I cannot recall now if I told you about Ginny's raise last January. She has been

May 10 1966 - Pages 1 & 2

promoted effective May 1st. She has more responsibilities now, that she is so nervous as she is also in charge of the petty cash. In a way I am glad for her, other times we are sad because she never really enjoy-ed much of her childhood. Sometime when I find the courage I may write you about our tribulation. Speaking of Ginny we thank God she is a good and patient girl - we always pray she will never change.

I have complained at our post-office of the non-delivery of the package I sent you as early as November. They have sent a tracer to find out what happened to it. It's a shame.

On Sunday we may go to Antipolo, a place famous for its waterfall. It is a small one but because it is the near-est one to Manila it is flocked to every May. I will send you a picture if we have one taken.

I am sending my kind regards to you and your family. We hope to hear from you soon.

Love,
Mercy

May 10 1966 - Pages 3 & 4

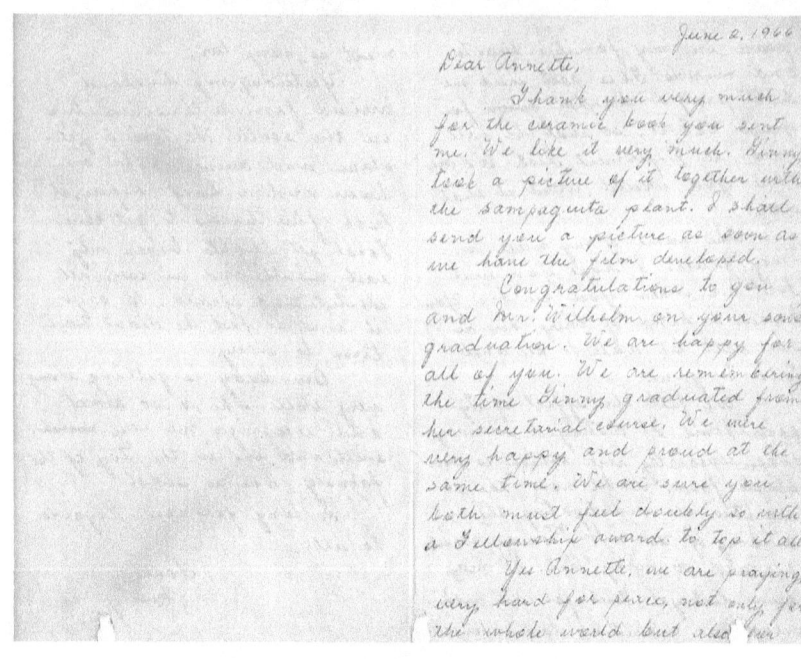

June 2, 1966

Dear Annette,

Thank you very much for the ceramic boat you sent me. We like it very much. Ginny took a picture of it together with the sampaguita plant. I shall send you a picture as soon as we have the film developed.

Congratulations to you and Mr. Wilhelm on your son's graduation. We are happy for all of you. We are remembering the time Ginny graduated from her secretarial course. We were very happy and proud at the same time. We are sure you both must feel doubly so with a Fellowship award to top it all.

Yes Annette, we are praying very hard for peace, not only for the whole world but also for

June 2 1966 - Page 1

peace in my family's hearts and minds. This past week we have prayed harder than ever for your Robert, so that he will pass the Deferment Test. We are sure you would want it that way.

The name of my niece is Emmy Jaleco. I hope you will like her when you see her. You know, I kind of envy her as she will be able to see and talk to you.

We felt the effect of Typhoon Irma. It destroyed so many crops, especially rice which is our staple food. Until now the authorities are investigating the sinking of the m/v Pioneer which claimed so many lives. It may seem disloyal but for an archipelago our maritime law enforce-

ment is very lax.

Yesterday my husband arrived from a business trip in the south. He took a jet plane and arrived after an hour and a half. Before, it took five hours to get there. Local jet flights began only last month and we were all excited and afraid. He says it was so fast he didn't have time to worry.

Our baby is getting along very well. She is so sweet and recognizes me very well and she is the joy of the family. She is sweet.

So long for now. Regards to all.

Love,
Nancy

June 2 1966 - Pages 2 & 3

Sept. 20, 1966

Dear Annette,

It was sweet of all of you to have gone and visited my niece Emely. I am very glad you liked her at once. She wrote her parents and me about your visit – she was very happy about it. She is in Philadelphia now and may proceed to New York with a friend. One of her sisters is here with me looking for a job as a dye chemist.

You say that Bob is working for Northrup and Leeds – I gather that he passed the Deferment List. We are very glad.

By the way, during your July 4th celebration did all the church bells ring? I read somewhere that there was a movement for all the bells to ring during your Independence Day except the Independence or Liberty Bell in Philadelphia because of the crack in it.

We used to celebrate our Independence day on July 4th too. Your country granted it on that day. But our last administration changed the date to June 12th for the reason that it is the date our countrymen proclaimed independence from Spanish rule. However not all of us favor the change. To this day, questions are still asked about the change.

Remember the Taal volcano that erupted last year? It erupted again for weeks although the damages were less than last year. Some newspapers have said the earthquake in Turkey had a direct bearing on its eruption.

Our President and First Lady are on a state visit in your country right now. Have you seen them on TV? If you heard our First Lady sing "Dahil sa iyo" which means "Because of you" —

Sept 20 1966 - Pages 1 & 2

did you like it? I mean the song. It is said that their visit brought rain to Washington D.C. In your state, did you have rain too? Here it is our season for rains and typhoons. We had three weeks of continuous hard rains that roads had to be weeded for almost a week. Our roads are so terrible now that some communities compare them to the surface of the moon. They do look like craters lately.

I am enclosing a picture of our south harbor in which is located Pier 13 reputed to be the longest in the world before the second world war. It is used for ocean going vessels. We also have a north harbor for inter island vessels. Also included is a picture of our Spanish church, the oldest in our country. It was the only edifice that stood the bombings during the battle of our liberation. Its walls are so thick it is like a fortress.

Before I close I would like to explain why I have not written for so long. I have not been well these past few months. According to the doctor it is the effect of years of anguish and worry that are now involved. The amazing thing is that now that it is all over, I feel its effect on my health. Such telltale signs were that often I could scarcely eat, I couldn't focus my sight and I lost interest in everything.

You recall perhaps that I never wrote you about my ——— activities. It was because of so evident that People here which acted in his leaving a revolutionary writer and according to the doctor a split personality. The first time I heard it, we felt that the heavens had fallen on our heads and that God had abandoned us. Speaking of that, you will perhaps notice that

Sept 20 1966 - Pages 3 & 4

the Lord never gives a Cross one
cannot carry." The day your letter
came was so timely as I was in
despair that day. My son was in
one of his violent moods and threw
a pair of shoes at my head that
made me fall. You'll never know
how you've helped me be resigned
to being resigned. my problem became
slighter. Since 1962 we had confined
them so many times. But our facilities are so inadequate. In a hospital for 2,000 people, 1,100 are
confined, that even in the pay ward
they accept only very violent men.

But it's all over now, thank
God, I am alright now and God
willing everything will be. The
doctors say, now it was a nervous
breakdown only.

God bless you.

Love Nancy
Sanchez

P. S. I was hesitant to confide
to you our problem as I did
not know how you will feel
towards me. But Emory says
you are very sweet in nature
as well as your family.

Same

Sept 20 1966 - Pages 5 & 6

122

Dec. 12, 1966

Dear Annette,

Do you know that I received your card before I got your letter? Our postal system is so terrible that a letter sent to my niece from the next municipality last August was delivered only last week. It is one of my country's biggest problems and the cause of much bickering among our congressmen.

It is 2 a.m. right now and the first time I can sit in peace and quiet. I am watching Mother (my sister-in-law) while she sleeps for the first time in days. She has been with me since her hospitalization last October. We are fourteen in the house now so you can just imagine the mess. Mother is in constant pain because of the bed-

Dec 12 1966 - Page 1

-sores and she can hardly talk nor swallow. As my home is very small I have placed her in the dining room and we use the kitchen instead. But we don't mind at all. We are happy to be able to take care of her and above all after our problem with our boy we consider these inconveniences as nothing because we have peace in our minds and hearts. We are all trying our very best to make Mother's last days happy and comfortable.

Last Nov. 16 I accompanied Linda to a TV station as she was scheduled to answer in a quiz program. At the last minute she became very nervous so I took her place instead. As luck would have it, I knew the answers. The answer to the first question was "the Seven Years' War"

Dec 12 1966 - Page 2

it is a "lucky partner' contest. As you can see in the clipping, my lucky partner is a 12-year older and he came with his parents the next day to claim his prize, #236 also. I picked his label from among the thousands which you can see in the background. That night was one of my happiest days. it was a family and friends reunion in our house. I felt like I won a million the way they made much of me. They were all happy for me that I cried for sheer joy to think that they all care. We did not even know it was published until we received the clippings from them as we subscribe to another publication.

For the first time since I was a little girl the last Thursday of Nov. was not declared a holiday. We used to celebrate Thanksgiving

Dec 12 1966 - Page 3

on the same day as yours. We are sure they are contemplating changing our Thanksgiving date.

Is it snowing there? Here the nights are beginning to be cold. Last night we put out our "Belen" in preparation for the Xmas Holidays. I read somewhere that in your country Christmas trees are taken down right after Christmas. Is it correct? Here you will be surprised at the length of the celebrations. We put up our trees on the 16th and take them down after the feast of the Three Kings which is on Jan. 6th.

I hope you will like the things I sent you especially the music which I am praying it will not be lost again.

Merry Christmas to You All!

Love
Nerry

P.S. Happy Birthday to your sister too!

Dec 12 1966 - Page 4

May 29, 1967

Dear Annette,

I must apologize for not writing to you for so long. I was quite ill for some time and right after I was well enough I was kept busy helping the boys with their term papers. I am so thankful that they all passed. Robert graduated from high school and Pierre his elementary studies. Robert wants to take up mechanical engineering. Speaking of graduation, I sent your Robert a congratulatory card last year. I guess it was lost in the mail.

We received the memento of your wedding anniversary and it made us feel we were there with you and your loved ones. Did you renew your vows in the church? Please send me some pictures if you won't mind.

You know we were married too

in 1942 but ours falls on July 11. It was to have been a simple wedding but the occupation made it simpler. We all walked to and from the church and because it rained hard after the ceremony we were all wet and cold when we reached home. We don't know if we will be able to celebrate our anniversary but we will surely go to hear Mass in thanksgiving and make certain that we will have some pictures taken. We had a camera then but no film and we could not afford a studio so we did not have a picture of our wedding.

The fall of Bataan was celebrated here last April 9th. Many of your countrymen came for the ceremonies and a sentimental pilgrimage to the forts they so bravely defended.

Thank you so much for the blouse and little things you sent me for my birthday. It is exquisite and just what I need as I have stopped wearing black because of the terrible heat which reaches 98° Fahrenheit almost everyday. We are afraid that if the rains do not come yet, by June our water will be rationed. As it is, almost everyone stores water in barrels.

I can't recall now if I had written you the washing procedure for the cloths you made into blouses. Please have them washed by hand as the washing machine will leave them frayed. Except for the design, the yellowish one is of pure pineapple fibers, the other one is interwoven with synthetic silk and both are handwoven.

Have you read Wm. Manchester's book "Death of a President"? It was

serialized in one of our newspapers. A Puerto Rican arrived here saying he was one of the plotters of President Kennedy's assassination. He is still being investigated.

At last my niece gave me some pictures and I am sending you one. The little boy looking straight to my nephew and a brother of the bride. Beside him is he. Beside me as she was the maid of honor.

The national costume I am wearing is a modernized one patterned after the trend now towards comfort. Before the war the skirt used to have a train which we held or pinned to one side. On top of the skirt we had a "tapis" usually of black tulle embroidered elaborately and augmented with sequins. We had also the "alampay" to shade over our necks to partly cover the butterfly sleeves. It was beautiful but uncomfortable.

Please say "hello" to your husband and son for me.

Love, Merry

Dear Annette,

How are you and your family? I thought you were still vacationing in Canada so I did not write sooner. Your package arrived yesterday so I knew you are home now.

Tony and I thank you all for your gift and appreciate very much your thoughtfulness.

As I told you we did not plan to celebrate our anniversary, as it coincided with the children's first day of schooling. But two nights before the occasion our friends brought birthday beer & wine for the women. My sister-in-law (Tony's only sister & our sponsor) came too with her gift - two white gold rings to be worn during the mass. We did not think they would remember. The

Aug 8 1967 - Page 1

priest renewed our vows in a simple ceremony. I had prepared meat with gravy, fish fillet, boiled macaroni, custard and fruit salad. My nephews and friends from the south sent crabs and fried chicken by air so we had more than enough for the gathering. All in all, we were fifty-eight in the house, even our bedrooms were full. Tony Jr. played the guitar, a friend the ukulele and we all sang and danced. Then alone, Tony & I danced to the tune of the Anniversary Song. I burst into tears. I couldn't help it - I was so happy. We were really destined not to have pictures and to be cold. My brother-in-law forgot to bring flash-bulbs & it was raining terribly hard. But we had a good time.

Do you travel to Canada by plane 'em or car? You are all busy

Aug 8 1967 - Page 2

to be able to travel so much. We
do our travelling in books and magazines and when the places we read
about are featured in TV we stop
everything and watch. TV is wonderful isn't it?

    Yesterday we went to one of Tony's
brothers to felicitate him. It is
the beginning of their birthdays.
We always say that it is one of
Ripley's "Believe it or not," because
the five brothers were all born in
August. Even my mother-in-law
was born in the same month.

    We read much of the riots in
your country. Was Baltimore affected too? Here we have peace
and order as the first and major
problem. I wonder if you read
of the snatching of one of our more

Aug 8 1967 - Page 3

stars, Maggie de la Riva. She is a
sweet girl supporting her family
by working hard at her career.
You can imagine my anxiety when
Ginny doesn't arrive early. We can
only pray and hope that peace
will prevail in all our countries.

    My niece Emey, has fallen in
love very much with your country, she wants
to stay. She sent me her papers asking a release from the Exchange
Program.

    Is Baltimore the capital of Mary-
land? I have always known it to be
so but my boys insist it is Springfield now. Sure enough, it is in
their case. So they told me to ask
the best authority on the subject.—
Mrs. Wilhelm.

    Our best regards to you all.
       Sincerely,
       Nancy

Aug 8 1967 - Page 4

www.ingramcontent.com/pod-product-compliance
Lightning Source LLC
Chambersburg PA
CBHW021647120626
46545CB00002B/743